DETOX
Your Mind

Also by Jane Scrivner
Detox Yourself

DETOX
Your Mind

JANE SCRIVNER

PIATKUS

© 1999 by Jane Scrivner

First published in 1999 by
Judy Piatkus (Publishers) Ltd
5 Windmill Street
London W1P 1HF

Reprinted 1999

The moral right of the author has been asserted

A catalogue record for this book is available
from the British Library

ISBN 0-7499-1885-3

Designed by Paul Saunders

Typeset by Action Publishing Technology, Gloucester
Printed and bound in Great Britain by
Mackays of Chatham PLC

To Dad and Mum and Kevin.
Thank you a million times for everything,
and for everything I have forgotten to
thank you for.

Also to Joyce, Pippa, Penel and Giles, Zach, Darcey, Chris and Catherine, Holly, Helen and Karl, Grace, Lilly, Sarah and Martin, Alban, Sophie and Jeremy, Georgia, Miranda, Kate and Aidan, Christian, Adrian and Kathryn, Kevin's Mum, Dad, Pamela and Donald, Amanda and Mark and Freya, David and Frances, Michelle, Anne and Russell, Ally, Carol and Kerry, who I think of often and I need to mention. Your reactions to *Detox Yourself* were fantastically and quietly appreciated and reminded me I should get excited about my personal achievements and draw strength from your support. Thanks.

Contents

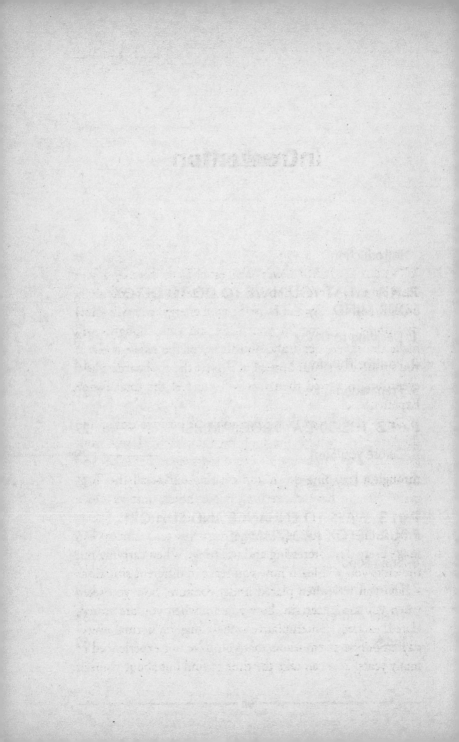

Introduction

Detox Your Mind was born out of *Detox Yourself*. If you have been through the process of cleansing your body in order to feel healthy and bursting with energy, you will know that doing the same for your head and your thoughts will make the experience truly 'holistic' – for the *whole* body. If you spring-clean your house but neglect the cupboards where everything is stored then you will not feel the total Detox Experience.

Detox Your Mind is a programme of positive doing and thinking. It provides the tools to completely cleanse your mind. You will follow a 30-Day Programme that takes you through a stripping-down and clearing-out of all the 'baggage' that we have cluttering up our heads: just as *Detox Yourself* strips your body of waste and toxins. The 30-Day Programme will actively change negatives to positives; will make every day interesting and uplifting. When carrying out the tasks you will learn how you react in different situations – how you feel when placed under pressure, how you seem when you are uncertain, how you act when you are scared, elated, excited, contemplative – these may be normal everyday emotions or emotions that you have not experienced in many years. You can take the time to find out about yourself and to be aware of yourself. You will discover if you generally go through thoughts and emotions without even registering them. After completing the programme there will never be another day on which you wish you had never got out of bed. If things aren't going your way or the way you want them to go then you can just look back at your tasks and remember how you felt before and after them and then realise that nothing can get you down. You are now able to think clearly enough to sort out any situation and strong enough to draw on personal resources to get exactly what you want! Every day will bring something new, something different, something to look forward to. You may even decide to get up earlier so that more can go right!

Only *you* can decide that you want to change from negative to positive; and only you can feel the wonderful benefits that come as a reward for all your efforts. Others will definitely notice the 'new you', but as only you get to see the view from the inside, so you will be the only person to know just how fantastic you are feeling.

When you decide to be more positive and clear thinking you are often faced with the question of 'how'? This question alone is enough to make your mind swirl and finding a way to move forward in a positive way *can* be quite daunting. It is made much easier if you are confident in yourself and your abilities. Not believing in your ability to carry out your new challenge is likely to stop you before you get the chance to start on your new road. The 30-day *Detox Your Mind* programme is an exercise in self-discovery and an exercise in believing in yourself. It will push you to do things you wouldn't think were possible. You will find that a little bit of success brings confidence and allows you to look at yourself in a more positive light. You will learn to believe in yourself.

With this new self-belief you can progress forward and decide how you want your life to be from now. If you know what you want in life and know exactly how to go about getting it, then everything you do will be to your advantage. You can work towards your goals on an everyday basis. If you can eliminate whatever stops you from focusing on your goals, then you will have more space and time to think about what you really want. Thinking about yourself isn't selfish; if you are happy and contented with your life, then your happiness and contentment will be passed on to others. We know that laughter is infectious – and so is moaning. We all know which one we would prefer to catch.

Happiness brings success and success brings happiness. Learn how to be successful and happy – Detox your Mind!

DETOX
Your Mind

Part 1

WHAT YOU HAVE TO DO TO DETOX YOUR MIND

1

Deciding to Detox

DO YOU NEED TO DETOX YOUR MIND?

If you answer yes to any of the questions below, then your mind is in urgent need of detoxing! This programme will get you back on the right track to a fully 'cleared-out' brain, ready for the arrival of fresh thinking and a new direction.

Do you daydream to get away from it all?

Have you forgotten to think about yourself recently?

Have you failed to do anything for yourself recently?

Do you think the cup is half empty, rather than half-full?

Do you have worries and niggles constantly on your mind?

Do you fall asleep worrying about the day that has gone and the day to come?

Do you feel that your thoughts are in need of organisation?

Is there something you would like to do but never seem to have the time?

Do your days and weeks come and go without much difference between them?

Do you want something to happen to you for a change?

Would you like to wake up in a positive frame of mind, looking forward to the day ahead?

Would you like to do something that you never dreamed possible?

Does your brain feel like the weather is always foggy?

Would you like your neighbourhood to be a friendlier place?

Do you know where you're at?

Would you like a reason to smile more?

Could you do with a good giggle?

Does the same old stuff go round and round in your head?

Would you like to change your world?

Detox Your Mind is a step by step guide to hundreds of ways in which you can explore, cleanse, refresh and revitalise the very corners of your mind so that it can work and think as efficiently as possible. What's more, you can have a lot of fun along the way, playing games with your own thoughts.

Mental health is just as important as physical health. But we never consider adopting a 'fitness plan' for our minds. We are all aware that we should exercise and eat the right foods to keep our bodies working well, but we don't do anything to keep our minds healthy and positive. All too readily we allow ourselves to see the bad or negative side of things. We never make ourselves examine the other side of the coin. We use our minds in the same way, day in, day out, never taking the time to look at things from a different angle, or to find a new challenge.

'Keeping mind and body together' means we should do just as much for our heads as we do for our hearts. *Detox Your Mind* will take you through games, exercises, nutrition, skills, complementary therapies and lots more ways in which you can 'spring-clean' your thoughts. Just reading the programme will give you a refreshing, positive mental boost.

You will discover skills you never believed you could possess and attempt things that may change the way you view your entire future. You will learn to change in such a way that your friends and family will see you in a whole new light.

The programme does not require amazingly high levels of intelligence or mental agility. It just requires you to open up your mind and 'have a go'. There are some things that may make you feel uncomfortable at first, and some things that may make you feel a little self-conscious, but everything is designed to get you to experiment with your self and 'clear those cobwebs'. Once you have become used to carrying out a few simple tasks each day, you will soon find that many of them will become habit. They will enhance your day-to-day life to such an extent that you will start doing them naturally, with no thought required.

The programme is divided into 'private' and 'public' tasks, which will be described at great length later on in the book. This means that a lot of the work you do, you are doing purely for yourself – no one need ever know. It is likely, however, that friends and colleagues will notice a difference in you almost immediately. It is then up to you if you want to spill the beans and spread the word.

The fact that you have already picked up this book means that you are likely to succeed in the programme, as your mind is all ready for a spring-clean. You are ready to clear your mind, banish the negative thoughts and start afresh.

THE PROGRAMME

The *Detox Your Mind* programme takes the form of 30 days and 30 tasks. Each day you can carry out a task or group of tasks that will make you look at yourself differently, look at your situation differently, look at others differently. Getting a new perspective on your life and your surroundings gives you the chance to think about what you want and what you don't want from them. We use our minds every day, and if they are cluttered then our thinking is cluttered. But if we can think clearly, then choices seem much more straight-forward. *Detox Your Mind* will help you to make decisions. You will learn how to say Yes to what you want and No to what you don't want without the usual hesitation and internal debates. It will stop your worrying and stressing over things you cannot do anything about, because your thoughts will be clear of everything but the essential or enjoyable.

You will feel challenged whilst doing the tasks, but euphoric once you have completed them. You will begin to use your mind in ways that you might once have considered too daunting, and this will alter your attitude towards all sorts of niggles and irritations. Problems will become challenges, exciting puzzles rather than insurmountable difficulties. You will approach absolutely everything with a positive perspective. Your old ways of thinking will be swept away and replaced with fresh, new outlooks.

Completing the 30 tasks will mean that you will have detoxed your mind within only one month. You can choose the month so it is the best timing for you. Start a new year with a detoxed mind; go into your exams with a positive perspective; start a new job ready for any challenge. Or just embark upon normal, everyday living with a whole new mindset.

We will look at the general areas that will be covered in the 30-Day Programme in the next few pages, so that you can get a feel for what lies ahead. The programme itself will thoroughly explain exactly what you should be doing each and every day. Try not to 'peek' at the tasks in advance – taking yourself by surprise is an important element in detoxing your mind. Some things may seem slightly strange when examined in isolation, but when they are in context within the Programme they will make perfect sense!

Self-Assessment

This is nothing to do with tax; it's a real chance for you to take a long, hard look at yourself. Once you have completed the 30-Day programme you will have carried out your own thorough self-assessment. You will have found out things about yourself that surprise and amaze you.

Usually we only take a look at ourselves when something has gone wrong, or when someone tells us to in the heat of an argument: 'I suggest you go away and take a long hard look at yourself!' As a result you might have resolved to be a 'better' person ... usually for no more than a day or two.

Following the *Detox Your Mind* Programme requires you to stop what you are doing and take a clear analytical look, not just *at yourself*, but *inside yourself* and *all around yourself*. Remember, this process can be completely private.

What you want in life

A Detoxed Mind is a clear thinking mind. Knowing exactly what you want in life means you can clear your head of questions about what you are doing and where you are going – if you *know* what you want, then every decision you make will be the right one. Part of looking at yourself, assessing your dreams and desires, is being truthful about what you want in life. Not just health, wealth and happiness – join the queue! – but much more specific things, things you can achieve immediately. You will be asked to think about what you really desire – *desire* is better than want because it injects passion, and passion is a strong motivational tool. Do you desire to live in the house you live in? Do you desire to re-plan the garden? Do you desire more friends or less friends? Do you desire to go out more? And so on. If you achieve your small desires then you are well on the way to achieving the big ones too. The programme will help you sort through your pile of wishes and dreams and focus on those you are really motivated to make come true.

Future planning

Don't waste your thoughts. Once you have decided what you truly desire, it is always good to do some real planning. If you have made proper plans, with target dates by which you intend to fulfil your aim, then you will be able to measure your achievements and check if you are on course to getting what you want. Having plans will prevent you wasting thoughts; having plans will mean that you know where you are going, that everything you do is focused on achieving your goals.

Living for the moment

Think about tomorrow, tomorrow! Future planning is important – but don't wish your life away! Living for the moment is great fun. You can be thoroughly fulfilled without doing anything other than living your life and feeling how it feels. Living for the moment means thinking about what you can do today. Don't waste mental energy today thinking about things you cannot do until tomorrow. How easy it is, when you have an exciting weekend ahead, to spend Monday, Tuesday, Wednesday, Thursday and Friday thinking about Saturday. Poor weekdays. What did they ever do to deserve being wished away? Your Saturday and Sunday are guaranteed. They aren't going anywhere, so why not enjoy the weekdays AND the weekend?

The big clear out

Our minds are fantastic. They contain all the information we need for going about the business of living. However, we also hold on to things we *don't* need. We bear grudges; we get jealous; we get annoyed that the bus didn't arrive on time; we worry that the bus won't come on Thursday; and so on. *Detox Your Mind* will examine the things you can do something about – and make you do it. It will also help you recognise the things you cannot do anything about and make you forget them, or file them away until you are able to tackle them. Worrying about something that may never happen, or has already happened, is exhausting and wastes energy. *Doing* something to stop you worrying is exhilarating – and a brilliant use of your time.

Who am I?

Are you true to your self? The only way to be true is to know who is the real you. Are you who other people think you are – or is there another side that you are scared to show. Can you change bits you don't want? Can you enhance bits you like?

Each task will help you on your way to discovering and understanding something new about yourself. Once the tasks have been completed you will know yourself: know how you feel, know what you want in life and how to go about getting it. You will know how to live in the moment, know how to clear out your personal junk, know how to keep what is valuable and use it to your advantage.

But it won't be easy. Sometimes you will feel exhausted, because you are using your mind in a way that it hasn't been used before. A breath of fresh air always makes you tired, but it is a *healthy* tiredness, a tiredness that comes from hard work and effort, not one that is born out of boredom.

Opening up new horizons and unlearning old habits

Many of our thoughts are old thoughts; like many old things they become out of date and inefficient. It is likely that, over the years, your brain has developed a set pattern of operation. A few adjustments to the way you think could change your life significantly.

We tend to pigeon-hole ourselves from a very early age. For example, we decide if we like arts or science when we choose our examination subjects at the age of 16 and we never seem to change that early opinion of ourselves. We decide that there are many things we couldn't possibly do; it just isn't our cup of tea. Restricting ourselves to what we *know* we are good at means that we eliminate millions of things that we could be brilliant at without even knowing it.

We limit ourselves on an everyday basis as well. Most people say that they are either a 'morning' person – 'I find the morning a really great time, it's all downhill after then', or an 'evening' person – 'I would say that I am at my best by about seven o'clock in the evening'.

See how we label ourselves? We run our lives according to what we think we know about ourselves and create our own personal, rigid rules and parameters. In order to detox your mind you must be prepared to forget these rules, eliminate any parameters – start afresh, update your thinking and clear your thoughts to focus on what is possible.

We will be carrying out certain tasks to find out which side of the brain works best for you. Was maths your subject at school, or did you decide to become a world-class footballer by the age of 18? Are you naturally logical and analytical, or are you imaginative and creative? How can you help yourself to try something different?

Whatever you are doing now – working, bringing up a family, not working – you *always* have the ability to try something different. Even if it is just in your head. Looking at things differently can bring a fresh new perspective on your circumstances or situation.

Detoxing your mind will encourage you to try something new, to dream about how things could be different and to actually *do* something different – something that may not necessarily alter your life beyond recognition, but may just alter the way you see things. A change is as good as a rest and it brings many more opportunities. And opportunities *always* have a positive outcome.

When was the last time you actually learnt something

new? Something which will bring about a change in your life? Once we leave formal education we tend to avoid learning at all costs. We might know how to do coloureds and whites in the washing machine, but we never try any other programme. We never bother to learn how to set the self-timer on the oven because 10 years ago the timer we had then was very unreliable and the turkey was stone-cold on Christmas day! We end up staying in to watch a programme on television because we still have not learnt how to programme the video. We look up our partner's number at work every time we use it. And we think it's impossible to commit to memory the PIN numbers for the numerous credit and cash cards we have in our wallets and purses ...

Learning to tackle any one of these tasks – or even beginning to think about tackling them – is, currently, not part of our personal agendas. But *Detox Your Mind* will make even the most complicated of tasks seem a refreshing challenge. You won't believe some of the things you are going to be doing! Once you have learnt something new your self-esteem gets a great big boost and you will start to see that you can try anything, that, for you, the impossible is now possible.

Getting out of your head

How often do you get out of your mind? I don't mean by taking illegal substances, but how often do you stop and look at what is around outside you. Inside our mind is where we spend most of our time. We are so preoccupied by our own schedules, by our own activities, that we cease to be aware of the rest of the world. If we can start to think about things that go on around us we will become more outward-looking, moving forward and taking on new challenges instead of staying still or slipping backwards. Looking outwards is enabling and active; looking inwards is dull and restrictive.

The programme will help you start to look at things outside your mind, your home, the shops you go to, the faces of friends, the faces of colleagues. You know the colour of your own front door, but do you know that of the house you live opposite? And what that might tell you about the dreams and aspirations of the people who live there? We miss so much by wrapping ourselves up in our normal lives. Seeking inspiration from outside our heads can only be a good thing – because it makes us think new thoughts. Introducing new information makes us challenge what we already know or do.

Get ready to start examining your internal thoughts and beginning to blend them with outside influences to produce an outward-looking, unique, whole-body experience.

2
Positive Thinking

DETOX YOUR MIND is an exercise in POSITIVE THINK-ING. Every one of the 30 tasks will show you how to look at things differently, with a more positive and forward-thinking frame of mind. Thinking about things positively will lead to a happier, clearer mind and a happier and healthier life.

We create the world from our own point of view.

If we think that we live in a depressing and disappointing world then we will end up depressed and disappointed. If we believe that these are the best of times and that we have never had it so good, then every day will be a good day, full of interesting happenings.

Simply rephrasing your thoughts can make the difference between a good life and a bad life!

NEGATIVE THINKING: EXAMPLES

- I didn't do as well as I could have done at school. I wasn't too bad at some subjects, but I was awful at others. Everyone seemed so much cleverer than me. When I left school I took the first job that came along – I thought I might not get offered another one. I didn't have the chance to think about what I really wanted to do.

- I always think that my colleagues could do my job better than me. The problem is that you can't teach an old dog new tricks and I simply don't have their skills.

- I was asked to go rafting the other day – not likely! It's something I've always fancied doing, but I'd only make a fool of myself.

- I was told off at work today. It really wasn't fair. They're always picking on me.

- Sally came home wearing bright yellow shoes the other day. I thought they were hideous – she's such an exhibitionist. I wonder if she realised how stupid she looked?

- David is going away again. He's never here for me – always off travelling and enjoying himself, whereas I just have to sit at home and watch TV, bored out of my mind.

- I got my bonus this month, but I don't have a clue what to do with it. I don't want to waste it, and if I spend it on a new outfit people will only say I'm trying to be flash.

- Things could be worse, I suppose, but you never know what's around the corner, do you? And I've got a family to worry about as well as myself.

and so on and so on, the picture gets very gloomy and depressing – this mind is closed and set in a rut. It is very easy to think in a negative way, we pass on negativity and then soon we feel life is really difficult – well it must be – just read the last few paragraphs – it sounds really awful – but there is nothing we can do, things are pretty awful …

Depressed? Disappointed? The person who wrote that certainly is! But if you 'think positive' the whole mood changes:

POSITIVE THINKING: EXAMPLES

- I did quite well at school. I was better at some subjects than at others – but that was OK, because it meant I learnt my strengths. There were lots of very clever people there and I wish them well. All their hard work paid off. When I left school I took the first job that came along. That was great because it meant I could get stuck into the real world immediately and find out what I liked and what I didn't. I really didn't know what I wanted to do, but that meant I was open to all suggestions.

- I always do the best I can at my job. If there is something that could be done better, then I will try and learn. Just because I would do something differently doesn't mean it is not as good – it means that I might find an even better way.

- I was asked to go rafting the other day – it fills me with trepidation, but what the heck! If I don't try now I may never get the chance again.

- I was told off at work today. It made me feel bad, but I didn't take it personally. I used it as constructive criticism, and I am going to try and improve so it doesn't happen again.

- Sally came home wearing bright yellow shoes the other day! I think she's terribly brave to wear them and though they aren't my taste they look great on her. She says they give her confidence – well done, Sally!

- David is going away again. It's great that he has the chance to travel such a lot, and it gives me the chance to stay in and perfect my DIY skills.

- I got my bonus this month and I'm going to spend it all on a new outfit – I deserve it! I'm really looking forward to going shopping.

- Things seem to be going well for me at the moment. I have a happy, healthy family and the future looks promising.

What a difference! The same information, but delivered in a much more positive state of mind. Supportive and non-judgemental where others are concerned; looking for the good points of personal experiences, learning from everything that happens.

WHAT GOES AROUND COMES AROUND

Good thoughts bring positive thinking and bad thoughts bring negative thinking. Good wishes bring luck and bad wishes bring gloom. If you smile at someone then they smile back – what you give out is what you get back. Once you have completed the 30-Day Programme you will find that smiling, positive thinking and good thoughts for other people become a normal part of your day. And if you give all these out, then they can only come back and multiply.

Using words in your everyday language that have a positive, uplifting feel will pass on positive and uplifting feelings:

yes	giggle
brilliant	smile
wonderful	snigger

great	fabulous
fantastic	gorgeous
amazing	beautiful
good	stunning
happy	charismatic
exciting	bright
fresh	lovely

Using words that are negative or have bad connotations will pass on negative, bad feelings:

no	down
dismal	stupid
unhappy	annoying
awful	uneasy
bad	stressed
stale	uptight
dull	frown
boring	shout
sad	horrible
melancholy	ugly

Our state of mind reflects very closely on our behaviour. If we are happy, then our behaviour is very different from when we are not. We are more likely to 'have a go' if our spirits are high and we feel able to try anything. If we feel depressed and lethargic it will be all we can do to get out of bed and get dressed, let alone go out and do something new, daring and exciting.

During the 30-Day Programme you must remain positive at all times to enable you to get the best out of every aspect and every day of the programme. You will be given tools to help you stay positive. You should spend the month continually assessing your state of mind; if things are getting you down, then a simple re-phrasing of your thoughts, and a few well-chosen affirmations should bring you back up to full positivity.

3
Preparation is key

THIS PROGRAMME is going to be something different for you. It is going to be a challenge. You are probably aware by now that the next 30 days are not going to be ordinary; they are going to be extraordinary. In fact you are about to embark on the most enlightening 30 days you have ever had! You will feel invigorated, refreshed and excited. You will start to see, even after the first few days, that by clearing out the clutter in your mind and allowing yourself to change, you can open up new horizons and make your head an altogether more positive place to be.

There are many ways in which you can enhance the programme and many ways in which you can make the tasks enjoyable and beneficial. Being in a relaxed and calm state of mind will make *Detox Your Mind* a pleasure to complete. The tasks will be natural and progressive; you should be able to slot them in to your everyday routine with ease.

To help you get the most from your mind we will look at **optimum nutrition** during the 30 days: at foods that will boost your alertness and alacrity, increase oxygen and nutrient supply to the brain and help you keep a clear head during the coming month. It's advisable to take meals at the times recommended to keep you fully awake and to keep your blood sugar as stable as possible.

Essential oils will play a large part in the 30-Day Programme. There are essential oils to cover all the moods and emotions that you may experience and this book contains a whole section dedicated to explaining how you can use the oils and which ones are good for what. The 30-Day Programme will be your very own course in personal aromatherapy. You are not expected to buy every oil described, but you are encouraged to choose the 10 oils that will serve your every need during and after the 30 days. The benefits of aromatherapy are not confined to the amazing fragrances – although these are often enough to clear your mind and banish negative thoughts – but extend to the in-depth effects they can have on every emotion, system and organ in the body.

A relaxed mind is an open mind, ready to receive new ideas, to look at things in a new light. **Relaxation exercises** are of massive importance during the programme. You will be requiring your mind to do some extra work over the next month, and the more relaxed you are, the easier it will be. The last thing you want is having to deal with existing stresses and strains in addition to handling new situations and challenges. Remember: anxiety is toxic, and this is a detox programme! There is a whole section at the back of the book designed to help you towards optimum relaxation, so that you can get the most from the programme.

Breathing is fundamental to life but we hardly ever breathe correctly. If we breathe correctly we will bring about optimum oxygenation of the blood, increase the blood's circulation and de-stress our bodies and minds. Breathing correctly is simple and can provide mental alertness on its own. Combine it with the programme and you will get the ultimate benefits.

Meditation and Yoga are the final steps you should take before you are fully equipped to get the best out of *Detox Your Mind*.

DETOX YOUR MIND SHOPPING LIST

There are some things that you will need prior to starting the *Detox Your Mind* programme. It is worth having these things to hand; you may find that without them you try and make do with something that is not quite right for the task and therefore not as satisfactory.

Notebook and pen	For making notes during the programme. These are likely to be quite personal and should be kept together. Scraps of paper are more likely to get lost or mislaid.
Diary	You will be asked to keep a diary during the 30 days. This could be the same book as your notebook; in that case you may want to use a bigger book so that you can use it both for your daily journal and your notes. You may also want to keep the notes you will make on all the tasks you do over the 30 days for reference; your own specially dedicated notebooks and diaries will make this more enjoyable.
Local information sources	Keep available copies of local newspapers during the 30-Day Programme. Have to hand a phone directory that will give you

details of local leisure centres, council offices, social clubs etc. Don't forget the local bus timetable and the local train timetable. All will be revealed later!

An appliance that you don't get on with! This will be required early in the programme. It should be something that you use on a frequent basis, but which has a number of functions which remain a mystery to you!

Relaxation music You can use ready-made relaxation tapes that have been made specifically for relaxation or meditation purposes, or you can choose something from your own collection. Instrumental music only is better than songs with lyrics, as these can be distracting.

Aromatherapy oils You will need to use some essential oils so you could find out in advance of that particular task where you can get good-quality essential oils at a reasonable price.

KEEPING A DIARY

Throughout the next 30 days you will need to keep a diary. This may be the same notebook you use throughout the programme, or you may decide to buy a separate diary and continue to use it even after the 30 days has passed.

You should make the effort to complete the diary each day. Writing things down puts the day into perspective and allows you to recall everything that happened; it also helps you to relax, knowing you have a permanent record of your ideas. Writing your thoughts down is like filing them tidily in an archive, rather than trying to store them in your head, causing clutter and confusion. You should read the diary as it stands to date every time you make a new daily entry. Reminding yourself about how you feel or felt will help you to decide what is relevant or meaningful, what is worth preserving for later reference.

Your diary is your personal record of your Detox programme. As you complete the tasks on each of the 30 days, the results may not become immediately apparent. Perhaps some of the tasks do not have an immediate impact; keeping a diary of events will ensure that you notice exactly when and how the effects are eventually felt.

You should use your diary as a detailed account of how you feel or think on every day of the programme. You don't need to describe getting up, having breakfast etc – but you do need to note how you are feeling in relation to any of the tasks you completed. Are you exhausted from all the unaccustomed extra thought; have you solved a problem because of any of the tasks; are you surprised or moved; has anything happened because of something you did earlier in the programme; have you made any decisions due to the tasks? Jot down anything outside your basic daily routine that happens during the 30 days, so that you can see how your mind is reacting and developing.

You should also note the tasks you enjoy and will choose to repeat regularly; those you find difficult; those you didn't get around to doing; those you didn't like at all. This will provide you with future reference if you follow the programme again; you will know in advance on which areas you need to concentrate.

Decide where is the best place to keep your diary. You should have access to it during the day so that you can jot things down as they occur to you or use it for reference. For this reason it shouldn't be too big or unwieldy. Something which can be carried in a pocket or bag is ideal.

When you make your daily entry you should do it at a quiet time. This diary is going to be your working document as you detox your mind and you should give it priority, care and attention. You are entrusting your innermost thoughts to it, so it should be treated with the utmost respect. Be sure to keep the diary in a private place. Your very personal thoughts and ideas may be misinterpreted if they get into the wrong hands.

Part 2

THE 30-DAY PROGRAMME

4

Before You Start

THE RULES

You have to follow the rules!

1. You must do the tasks in the order that they are given. They are structured so that every part of your brain is used in the first few days and developed as the month progresses.

2. You must do *all* the tasks. You cannot leave out the ones you don't like the look of – they are likely to get the best results.

3. Start the tasks on a day which allows Day 8/9 to fall on a weekend (or when you have 2 days off).

4. Keep a diary throughout the programme – this will provide a permanent record of how your thoughts are becoming more positive. It will also store all your thoughts so your head can remain clear, ready for the next stage.

5. You must actively participate in each task, analysing at every stage how you are reacting, how you are actually 'feeling'.

6. Don't 'peep at' the tasks too far in advance. The element of surprise adds to the effectiveness of the task. The tasks are intended to keep your brain on its toes! Perhaps you could set aside a time to study each task the day before you are due to carry it out.

7. Enlist a friend or colleague to do the programme with. Discussion will help you to discover much more about yourself and how your thoughts, desires and reactions differ from those of other people.

8. Read through the Brain Food section before you commence the programme. This will enable you to include 'brain food' in your daily diet and get optimum nutrition during your mental detox.

THE TASK DIRECTORY

Day 1   Smiling

Day 2   Establish some 'me' time

Day 3   Use your creativity

Day 4   Perceived risk taking

Day 5   Teach an old dog new tricks

Day 6   Floating day

Day 7   Listen to yourself

Day 8/9   Use your imagination

Day 10   Find out how people see you

Day 11   Make some room in your head

Day 12   A change is as good as a rest

Day 13   Change as a catalyst

Day 14   Get some therapy

Day 15   Make their day – and yours

Day 16   Positive thinking

Day 17   Dreams and wishes

Day 18   Learn 5 new things

Day 19   Your 5-year plan

Day 20   Silence is golden

Day 21   Back to basics

Day 22   Floating day

Day 23   Brain boosters

Day 24   Self-esteem

Day 25   Draw your day

Day 26   Affirmations and visualisations

Day 27   Change your mood

Day 28   Floating day

Day 29   Your personal mantra and meditation

Day 30   A time for reflection

Once you have completed a task you must tick it off your list. Clearing items from the list signifies that you are clearing them from your mind.

Before you start ...

Today is the first day of the rest of your life.

In 30 days' time you will know your mind. You will have used your mind in new and very different ways. You will know what is in your mind and how you wish to expand its use.

- You will have confidence

- You will conquer negative thinking

- You will beat stress and worry

- You will discover your own feelgood factor

- You will boost your creativity

- You will 'use your head' more effectively

- You will clear your mind of clutter

- You will feel more relaxed and peaceful

- You will believe in Number One

You are unique. No one else even comes close to being like you. You are fantastic, imaginative, creative, caring, generous, happy, bright and cheery. Nothing is beyond your capability and no challenge can defeat you. If your mind is positive and open, you can achieve anything. *Detox Your Mind* will teach you how to keep your head clear and focused – the next 30 days will prove to you that your mind can be as clear and active as you want it to be.

From this point absolutely anything can happen. You will be able to do what you want – and do it successfully. And it will feel great when everything goes just the way you planned!

Remember: only you can do things the way you do them. You have your own individual style, that makes your life yours and no one else's.

You do your job in a way that is special to you alone; your family and children love and respect you – unconditionally; your friends know they can rely on you for wisdom and advice; your partner and friends will always be there for you; strangers think you are friendly and approachable, worth getting to know.

You are totally down to earth. No airs and graces – what you see is what you get where you are concerned. You have no hidden agenda – just hopes and desires, and a determination to get what you want in life. *And if anyone deserves that, then you do.*

All of this might sound wildly exaggerated to you. You may feel it doesn't apply to you. It's true that each person is different – but there's also an element of truth for everyone in all of the above statements. If they weren't true, you wouldn't have bought this book! If you learn to believe one hundred per cent in yourself and your capabilities, then you are free to conquer the world.

Self-esteem and self-belief are the strongest personal tools you can possess. If you believe in yourself and in the potential of your own mind; then well done – you are well on your way to a truly Detoxed Mind.

For the next 30 days you are going to take part in an entertaining, light-hearted, good long look at yourself. You will see what goes on in your mind when asked to do something that makes you uncomfortable, or something that you enjoy. Some tasks will make you challenge what you have taken for granted for the whole of your life; some will make you decide to implement some major changes for the future.

All the tasks are geared towards clearing out mental clutter, or 'toxins'. The things that inhabit your mind through force of habit, because you haven't taken the time to deal with them, or because you haven't ever given them much thought.

So off you go – *Detox Your Mind*!

5

The 30-Day Tasks

Day 1

SMILING

Smiling is positive. It gets any conversation or encounter off to a good positive start. Thoughts are uplifted and problems seem easier to deal with if you smile. Ease your thoughts with a smile!

I recently read that children smile an average of 400 times a day, whilst adults only manage to crack a grin 15 times a day. It seems a shame that something so simple – something children can manage to do without thinking 400 times a day – seems to be so hard for us. We get out of the habit of smiling; there is so much else to think about, so much that is serious and doesn't seem to warrant a smile. But why not be serious with a smile? If you smile when doing a task, the task seems lighter, less arduous; if you frown the task becomes an unhappy, negative experience. If someone smiles at us we automatically seem to smile back. It makes us feel good.

So today, Day 1 of your Programme, you will smile at everything that deserves a smile.

- Smile at the bus driver and thank him for your ticket

- The first shop you go into, look at the shop assistant and say hello with a smile. When you leave, say goodbye and thank you – and smile

- When you pick up the phone, say your number or name, hello or good morning, with a smile

- If anyone opens a door for you, say thank you and smile. Hold the door open for the person behind you – and smile

- If you are reading a business document, then exchange your usual dour look of concentration for a smile. It will intrigue the people around you about the content of what is a serious, dull report! Not to mention making your read more interesting

- Write your shopping list with a smile. Think of all the fabulous foods you are going to buy: fragrant bread, delicious pasta, earthy potatoes. Smile, and an everyday task can become a joy

Smiling is catching. There is nothing more likely to make you giggle than someone who is giggling uncontrollably themselves; there is nothing more likely to make you smile than someone giving you a great big grin. Even if you find the Laughing Policeman incredibly old-fashioned, you are still likely to have a little chuckle to yourself.

The main thing to remember with smiling is that you have to look as if you mean it. If you sit in front of a mirror first thing in the morning before your 'smile-in' and simply make the shape of a smile, you will see that it looks unconvincing and awful: the sort of smile you get from a tired shop assistant, going through the motions. Smiling needs to be genuine. A real smile will light up your face, crinkle your eyes and wrinkle your nose, it will show your teeth and lift your cheeks; and it will make you feel *great*. It comes from nowhere and knocks 'em dead and a true smile will almost certainly be returned within seconds of being given.

So try a few out – just to remind yourself how good you look when wearing a smile – and then you are fully prepared for the day ahead.

Important things to remember

The smile must be genuine Try saying something nice about the person in your head as you smile and this will ensure the smile is real

Check the response of the person to whom you give your smile See how many times your smile comes back at you

Keep a diary Write down how you felt about smiling all day. Was it exhausting or uplifting? Did it feel strange or did it feel natural? Did you enjoy it? *Did it make you smile?*

Day 2

ESTABLISH SOME 'ME' TIME

You are the most important person in your life. If you aren't happy, then it becomes very hard to generate any happiness for others. Grab some 'me' time and watch your thoughts relax with you.

During this 30-day period you will spend each day or a section of each day thinking about yourself doing things for yourself. This is something that we are not normally encouraged to do. Indeed, it is frowned upon – it is considered selfish, self-centered!

Well, there's good news. You should start to include time every day during which you do something *for yourself*. It can be frivolous, or serious, but it must be entirely for you. No one else.

My mother had a great phrase; she would insist on 'Having a me'. That meant that she would go off alone and do something which we knew, as children, it was totally taboo to interrupt. It was usually something like taking a bath that lasted longer than 5 minutes, or it could be an extravagant half-hour to read the paper with a cup of tea and a biscuit – but whatever it was, it was *her* time, dedicated to her alone. The result was that she would emerge calmer, less frazzled, more open to suggestions.

'Me' time should be, officially, part of your life. It is chilling-out time; you can use it to put a full stop on to what has gone before and a capital letter on what is to come. It is a time to gather your thoughts, concentrate on yourself and your feelings. You lead a hectic life, with many different demands on your energies – for a short period each day, you're entitled to shut those demands out and indulge yourself.

It is important that you do this every day. If you put it off, or try to take 2 hours every 4 days, then, believe me, your 'me' time will slip and disappear. Ideally your 'me' time should take up at least twenty minutes:

- have a cup of tea and a biscuit

- apply a face pack

- visit a golfer's driving range
- read a magazine from cover to cover
- watch a programme you recorded
- go for a walk around the block
- balance your cheque book
- stroll around the garden
- write a letter to a friend
- clear your handbag out
- clean your car

As you can see, none of these things will change the world. But at first, if you aren't inspired, you can use your 'me' time to complete all those little jobs which would improve your quality of life – but which, somehow, you never find time to do. Then, when they are all finished, you can start to really use your imagination as to how to spend your daily 20 minutes of 'me' time.

Day 3

USE YOUR CREATIVITY

Getting your thoughts to come to life in writing or pictures makes them easier to understand.

Today you will draw a picture and write a poem about what's going on in your head.

This is not going to be a potential work of art; it is simply intended to be a representation of what is there. The picture should use colours and shapes to communicate your innermost thoughts. I don't want to suggest what you might draw, because that would mean that I am impressing my own interpretation upon your mind, but if you think about children's drawings then you will get the idea. Children use yellow to signify warmth and brightness. They use black for what is scary and bad. They use big swirly circles to mean speed. Children instinctively grasp basic symbols and signifiers.

Your drawing should be private. It may develop into a series of drawings; you can do them in your diary or notebook or you can use bigger sheets of paper to express what is in your mind.

The drawings children do are very truthful – sometimes frighteningly so. Make your drawings just as truthful and you will learn a lot about what is going on inside your head.

The other part of today's task involves poetry. It works exactly the same as drawing, and you may find it easier or harder to execute – but you must try both. With pictures you use colours and shapes to express yourself; with poetry you use words. Keep the words simple. When you write about feeling happy or angry, use those words. Don't feel you have to be a literary genius. Your poems do not need to rhyme and they do not need to 'scan' – just get your thoughts down on paper at random.

The following is an example of how someone who was very busy put down in words what was going on in their head:

Too fast too bust
everything is a bit fuzzy
very exciting but I'm not sure I'm up to it all. I'm sure they will
*   let me know.*

Sore throat, am I overdoing it, no that's an excuse,
just do it, really really enjoy it and then carry on.
unbelievably exciting now but terrifying really
I need some sleep

As soon as the poem was down on paper the writer felt relieved. Thoughts that she had suppressed were now 'out of her head' and down on paper; and it was easier for her to get a perspective on how she really felt.

Now it's your turn. As you can see, no skill is required – just tell it like it is.

As with the drawings, you should keep a few of your poems and then read them to yourself over a period of time. Read 'good' poems when you feel bad, to remind you that you can feel better.

Keep returning to the drawings and poems throughout the programme, if you find them helpful. You may only want to do one or two today; don't force the issue. If you hit writer's/painter's block, then stop, get on with your everyday activities and wait until you're feeling more creative.

Believe me: there is no question that you can do this. You're not looking for a masterpiece. The drawings and poems will simply help you understand what is going on in your head. They will help you to self-knowledge.

Day 4

PERCEIVED RISK TAKING

Nothing concentrates the mind like a small dose of abject terror! You can find out so much about yourself – how you feel, how you react – in just a few short moments.

Detox Your Mind is not about putting you at risk. Far from it. It is about protecting you from what is unnecessary and irrelevant. But putting yourself through an extreme experience (with all safety measures observed so that the actual risk is only perceived) is a very effective way of finding out what is really important to you. This will help you prioritise your desires.

So why not do something you would never normally dream of doing? Something that, possibly, terrifies you? You may say to yourself, OK, that's enough. I've come this far, I'm going back now – I can't even believe I'm doing this much! Then you find out that not only have you done it, but that it was fantastic, amazing, exhilarating, and gave you more confidence than you ever dreamed of. Enough to make you believe that you can do anything you want to if you put your mind to it.

Perceived risks can be taken by going along to a place where there are professionals equipped to take you through an unusual experience whilst observing all the correct safety rules and guidelines. They will also assess whether you are fit and able to carry out the task without putting yourself in any real danger. The risk will all be in your head.

You might want to consider the following:

- Assisted parachute jump
- Bungee jumping
- White-water rafting
- Rock/Wall climbing
- Balloon trip
- Glider flight

- Holding a snake

- Holding a tarantula

- Go-Kart racing

- Mountain biking – on mountains

- Cave diving

- Scuba diving

- Horse riding

- Public speaking

- Appearing in a play

The list goes on … It is hard to name everything that would fit into this category. As you can see, it doesn't have to put you in physical danger. But it does have to be something which you, personally, find daunting.

Important things to remember

Work out for yourself what would be your biggest challenge. Then, when you feel ready, make the necessary arrangements.

Call the association or club that operates the risk of your choice and find out as much as you feel you need to know. There are some helpful telephone numbers in your local phone book that should get you started.

Once you have found something that you would like to have a go at, and that fits your budget and your timing, then book yourself a place!

Obviously this is a lot to get done in one day. Use Day 4 to start to think about the project – there will be time on subsequent days to check that you are making progress with this part of the programme. Use one of the spare 'floating days' to carry out your task.

Good luck – and fingers crossed!

When you put your mind to something and truly focus your thoughts – is there anything beyond your reach?

David was attending a weekend camp. Part of the activity was about facing a big challenge. The camp was geared towards providing facilities like rock climbing and mountain biking to enable people to confront their fears and 'deal' with them. David's challenge was to climb a 25-foot telegraph pole and then jump off the top! The exercise was purely a mental challenge; he was fully supported by a harness, and his team mates were holding the ropes, so there was no real physical risk involved in the process at any stage.

But David was scared of heights. The idea of climbing a pole that was 25-foot high and then jumping off the top was an horrific one to him. Through the process of getting to know his team mates and finding out about their fears and doubts, he began to set his mind at rest a little. He had assumed that the challenge would be easy for everyone except himself, but he found that this was not the case and that every single person had a doubt or anxiety about some part of the challenge.

Once the team had been briefed it was time to put on the harness and begin the challenge. Each team member was asked how they wanted their fellow members to support them and how much encouragement they needed. David was terrified, but as he watched his team-members climbing the pole and listened to the encouragement and support they received, he began to feel that perhaps he would climb the pole but turn back at the top, as that was more than he had ever thought possible.

David's turn came. He asked his team to designate one person to shout encouragement. When he gave the word he would be open to any words of wisdom. As he climbed the pole he kept saying to himself, '*One more step, just one more step*'. About halfway up he was going to stop, be satisfied he had done this much. He got more support from his team and then took a few more steps. Then he reached the top. This was more terrifying than anything he could ever have imagined. Not only was it high, but the top plate actually moved. He froze, but then he heard a voice from below, telling him just to breathe deeply and start to place one foot on the disk and then push his weight onto his foot. And then he was standing on the top, holding on. He released his hands slowly and began to straighten up. The pole began to sway and everyone shouted to him to concentrate on his breathing; hard as it was he did some really deep breathing and the pole became still. The language coming from David's mouth was very strong but his sheer euphoria about actually being there was unimaginable. If he could do this, then he could do anything because nothing else could come close to being on the top of a 25-foot pole when you are scared of heights. Except, maybe, jumping off the pole … The team began to tell him it was time to jump. David called back – 'I can't jump, but I am going to step off. I am stepping off a 25-foot pole into oblivion but I'm trusting you guys to take my weight.' David stepped off and his whole body lurched into his mouth, as if he had jumped off his life as he knew it. Within a split second – that felt like a day – his team members took the weight and he was swaying in mid-air, safely in his harness.

His feelings when he reached ground were something that he could never describe. But he had done something that changed the way he would think about himself for the rest of his life. By simply focusing his thoughts on what he wanted to do, and banishing all negative thinking, the outcome could only be positive. There was nothing beyond his reach!

Day 5

TEACH AN OLD DOG NEW TRICKS

Doing an activity that you consider beyond you is a challenge that will result in a boost of self-esteem and some exercise for your grey matter.

Learning a technical function means that you are likely to need the help of a willing friend or the help of an instruction manual – those things that usually get filed away safely when the appliance arrives and then never see the light of day until you need the guarantee for the repair man!

You may be one of those people who love to take apart your CD player of a weekend and then put it back together again with no problem whatsoever. That's great, and you may now take the rest of the day off. But spend your time wisely by going through the list of 'perceived risks' and finalising your choice, or making the last few arrangements before your big day.

If, however, you are one of the many millions to whom technology is a mystery, a complete no-go area then today is your day.

Choose an appliance that has always been incomprehensible to you:

- The video recorder
- The timer on the oven
- The memory on the telephone
- The diary on your personal computer
- Spreadsheets on your personal computer
- Printing labels on your personal computer
- Storing numbers on your mobile phone
- Checking the oil and water in the engine of your car

Once you have chosen your appliance, then choose the function that to date has been ignored or, alternatively, labelled as 'someone else's job' – and, quite simply, teach *yourself* how to do it. If at first you don't succeed, then just breathe deeply and try again.

Important things to remember

Make sure you have all the relevant parts. If a vital piece on your appliance is missing or broken, then no matter how you try, you will find it impossible to get any results.

Make sure you are solving a problem that you *want* to solve. If you never use the video, or never need to put the oven on the timer, then there is little satisfaction in learning the process if you never get the added thrill of using it.

Make a mental note of how your task will make your life easier and less complicated:

- You can go out more as you will be able to record important programmes in your absence

- You can go out on Sundays for long relaxing walks and come back to the smell of a delicious roast dinner

- You can call all your friends and tell them your news with the minimum of effort

- You won't need to go to your handbag every time you want to know if you have a free slot in your diary

- You can put all your personal/work finances on your spreadsheet – you will never be overdrawn again!

- Sending letters to colleagues or friends will now be less of a chore

- You can look ahead to years of secure, confident motoring

Make a mental note of other things that you could do in the technical field to save time and effort – and make a date to do them.

Don't be afraid to join the 21st century. Technical advances are designed to make your life easier and trouble-free – don't be baffled by what seems new and strange at first. If you can learn to make technology work for you, you will free up time for doing other, more important things. If you are in control of your technology, you will use it with total confidence – it will even give you pleasure. Finding solutions to problems, and discovering new skills, can only give you more opportunities.

Day 6

FLOATING DAY – *TAKE A BREAK!*

You can use today to plan your Perceived Risk Taking in greater depth; or you can simply read your diary and assess the progress you have made so far. Are the clouds lifting from your mind? Are you discovering new interests and enthusiasms? Are you more receptive to ideas? Have you learnt anything new? Are you beginning to feel detoxed: sharper; more sure of what you want; more confident; more positive?

Day 7

LISTEN TO YOURSELF

Detoxing is about getting rid of waste and toxins and getting more of what is good for you. In *Detox Your Mind*, the waste and toxins are the negative thoughts and the self-imposed limitations of your mind; the goodness is whatever is positive, upbeat, happy. So becoming happy and positive yourself is essential. Start by finding out how you really think and feel about yourself.

Today you must get to know yourself. Your self. You may think that this is odd; given that you are your 'self', then surely you know everything about you that there is to know? Not true. Usually you take your 'self' for granted.

Every day you carry out tasks and jobs without question. But how do you really feel about them? And has your body told you how *it* feels?

When I say you should listen to yourself, I mean you should learn to recognise your instinctive responses to situations. Learn how to assess what you *really* feel. Every day we do many things that, if we took time to listen to our response, we would not do – or would do differently. Listening to yourself involves being honest about what you really want. If someone calls you and says they are about to buy a new suit, but would like a second opinion, chances are that you are halfway out of the door and on the way to the shop before they have finished speaking. But listen to yourself – is that what you really want to do? Did your heart sink when you first heard the request? Did you tell yourself that it wasn't convenient, that you were too busy – and then automatically reject that assessment for fear of being thought rude? Perhaps you really are too busy. Perhaps you will be in a more helpful and constructive mood tomorrow, when you are less rushed.

Your body can also tell you truths, if you listen to it properly. Perhaps you know that you need to go to the gym – so you pack a bag and stagger off to complete a workout. But did you listen to those protesting muscles, telling you that they hadn't yet recovered from yesterday's workout? Exercise *now* will be an unpleasant chore, something to be endured, not enjoyed, and you may even end up putting too much strain on your body – but exercise *tomorrow* will be fun, invigorating and a great tonic.

(NB: listening to yourself is not simply an excuse to procrastinate and put off the things you don't much like doing! If you *really* listen, your mind and body will tell you how essential they are ...)

Listening to yourself carefully will also give you a much deeper understanding of how you really feel about yourself and the true nature of your desires and responses. One excellent way in which you can get yourself into the habit of 'listening' is by writing yourself a letter. If you do this without giving too much deliberation to every word you write – let the prose flow as a 'stream of consciousness' – the results can really surprise you.

Here is a passage from a letter written by a person to her 'self'. The person in question believed at the time that she was a little overweight; she thought constantly about eating less and exercising more. The letter was written after a relaxation session, when the writer's mind had been freed to be honest:

As I reflect upon my relationship with my body I feel comfortable and healthy and progressive. I feel that I have a working relationship with my body, that I am working towards a natural balance – it is give and take. Sometimes I reward my body and sometimes it rewards me. I am enchanted by its boundless capability – much, I believe, is yet to be realised, and this is exciting. I know my disappointments in my body are transient and superficial . . .

Once you begin to get in touch with how you really feel you will find that your own letter will be just as personal and emotional. One thing is for sure: it will certainly make you assess yourself differently. In this case the writer discovered that she actually liked her body a lot more than she realised. Now that she had taken time to listen to her self she realised that all her concerns were really unimportant and that she was actually proud of her body.

The writer then gave her 'body self' the chance to respond to her 'mental self':

Relax. Do not try to change things. We are working at a pace that is natural and we will get there in our own time.

Let the fluctuations go by, don't 'need more control' – I am happy that we are working together. I will listen more to your requests and signals without trying to change them...

Upon reading this through, the writer found that she had come to an agreement with her 'self': *live and let live and things will work themselves out*. The writer was also surprised at how much respect she had for herself deep down – something she had never realised before writing the letter.

As a result, instead of the relentless tussle she was having between eating less to get a fitter, leaner figure and being happy with her perfectly acceptable body – a debate which takes up a lot of space in your mind – she began to relax more. She became more contented with the way she was. This meant that she had loads of space and time in her life to get on with enjoying herself.

Preparation for talking to yourself

For the Programme you need to write a wide-ranging letter that allows your 'self' to say how you are really feeling, what you want to feel, what's causing you concern and what is good about your life. Basically, anything that is currently in your head.

You will need a quiet, warm room for an hour or so, together with a notebook and pen – or your *Detox Your Mind* diary. In order to get the best out of this task you should precede your session with a relaxation exercise (see Part 3). You may like to play a tape of calming music – make sure it is music only, as lyrics are likely to cloud your thoughts. Alternatively your relaxation tape may have a pre-recorded exercise on it; this is ideal as you can simply follow the tape.

Once you have completed your relaxation exercise it is time to start to write. Take your pen and write a letter to your self. Be very honest; don't try and analyse or censor how you are feeling. Just tell it like it is, now, today. Remember – no one but you will ever see this letter.

Once you have completed the letter then sit back, breathe deeply and then read it to yourself, slowly. The letter will deserve a response; you have put a lot of emotion into your letter to your self. So write back and say how you feel after reading the letter. Did it surprise you? Did it shock you? Did it reveal feelings you didn't know you had? Have you uncovered problems you weren't aware existed? Did it show you have strengths you'd never previously recognised?

Once you have completed today's task you will have found out much more about who you are. You will have cleared out things you now know to be irrelevant, and kept the things you have decided are important. You won't have solved all your difficulties but you should have them in a new perspective.

Well done – you now have 'space' in your mind to move forwards.

Days 8 and 9

USE YOUR IMAGINATION

It is very easy to spend money on entertainment without even thinking. It is very easy to spend money on keeping yourself occupied without even thinking. If we wake up and think 'what should I do today', one of our major considerations is how much money we have got. If we have a lot –

say, at the start of the month – then we have more choice of activity than at the end of the month when funds are running low. If we have no money, we tend to think we cannot do anything; if we have had a windfall or a win on the lottery then we can do absolutely anything.

But having money to do things stops us from considering other options. We are told, by the media and advertisers, that you can only have fun if you have money. This is just not true. There are millions of things that you can do to keep occupied, or to entertain yourself that cost nothing.

For the next 2 days of the programme you are going to detox your mind of all the short-cuts to happiness. You are going to give some thought as to how to spend your time without spending your money.

The 'shopping' list at the beginning of the book told you to obtain local papers, a bus timetable and a train timetable. Checking out other sources of information – your local library, shop windows, council offices, community and sports centres – can also be very helpful.

Planning and, conversely, spontaneity are the key to the success of these 2 days: planning to make sure you have the items from the shopping list to hand; and spontaneity to allow you to use your mind to find substitutes to the normal costly activities we use to pass our spare time.

To give you an idea of what you can and cannot do, here is a list of things which are out of bounds as they are either expensive or do not encourage you to use your imagination or brain power. They are 'supplied entertainment'. 'Use it or lose it' is very relevant when it comes to entertaining yourself. If you are creative and ingenious where your free time is concerned, this attitude will be transferred to other areas of your life.

- Renting a video
- Going to the cinema
- Going to the theatre
- Going out for dinner
- Going shopping
- Going to the zoo
- Going for a drive
- Meeting friends for coffee
- Going to the pub

The following activities cost nothing and are very definitely permitted. Some of them are unusual and will need real imagination and resourcefulness.

- Using storecupboard ingredients to make a cake
- Using storecupboard ingredients to cook a meal for friends
- Weeding the garden
- Exploring your local area
- Decorating a room
- Tidying a cupboard
- Reading about a new topic at your local library
- Relaxing with natural face packs and home beauty exercises; teabags on eyes, cucumber on eyes, salt scrubs, cold showers etc
- Drawing or painting a local scene or landscape

- Volunteering for a local hospital or charity

- Sorting out all your old clothes and donating them to a charity shop

- Making a patchwork quilt from clothes which are too shabby to sell or give away

- Reading a book

- Visiting a friend you haven't seen in ages, who lives within walking distance

- Sewing buttons on where needed

- Fixing everything around the house that you have already bought the spare parts for but have not yet found time to repair

- Camping out in your back garden

And so on. Notice: the list of activities that cost nothing is much longer and much more interesting than the list of things which will cost you money!

Important things to remember

Try to do only minimal preparation, to make your 2 days seem more spontaneous. If you think about the 2 days too much in advance you may subconsciously plan ahead – the real challenge to your self and mind is to come up with exciting, original alternatives on the spur of the moment.

Try and be sociable. Don't think that you have to become a recluse for 2 days just because you have no funds. Encourage your friends to join your challenge; they should be your entertainment, not just people that you spend money with.

Make a mental note of how you react to being less dependent on what money can buy. What does this tell you about yourself? Is it unnerving, or exciting? Is it tiring, having to use your mind to entertain yourself, or is it inspiring? Have you completed tasks that have been hanging around forever, or did you use your time to try out totally new activities? Ask yourself if you will try this again in the future.

If you are using money instead of imagination, try to exercise your brain cells to get your entertainment. Clear out the 'short-cuts' to fun and nourish your thinking!

Day 10

FIND OUT HOW PEOPLE SEE YOU
Do your friends see you the same way you see yourself? Do they see your strong points? Do they see a positive person, or do you seem to show them your more negative qualities?

Today you will find out how other people see you and how it compares to how you see yourself. If you give out a positive 'vibe', then your thoughts are probably well on their way to getting thoroughly detoxed; if you give out a negative 'vibe', then some more work on clearing out your negative thoughts is required. This process will require honesty, so you should select 3 or 4 friends who are prepared to be honest in the name of research!

Simply asking what people think of you will never give you the results you want. Getting in-depth, detailed information requires questions cleverly crafted to get you thinking about the sort of person you are. Questions which are easy to ask and to answer.

Once the questions are answered you should not debate or revise the replies with the person you have asked. Their first answer will be the most spontaneous and therefore the most truthful.

Firstly you must ask yourself the same questions that you ask your friends. Jot down your answers and don't leave out the second part of the question; this will help you decide if the answers you get from your friends are the same or different from the answers that you gave.

Once you have done this then contact your friends, ask the questions quickly (it may be better to call your friends on the telephone and ask them out of the blue, to stop them from preparing the answers they think you will want to hear). Choose from 3 or 4 of the following:

Question: If I was a car, what make of car would I be?
(Let them answer and then use the answer to ask the next question)
Answer: Mini Metro
Question: What type of person is a Mini Metro-type of person?

Question: If I was a colour, what colour would I be?
(Let them answer and then use the answer to ask the next question)
Answer: Yellow with blue dots
Question: What type of person is a yellow-with-blue-dots-type of person?

Question: If I was a piece of fabric, what kind of fabric would I be?

(Let them answer and then use the answer to ask the next question)
Answer: Red gingham fabric
Question: What type of person is a red-gingham-type of person?

Question: If I was a country, what country would I be?
(Let them answer and then use the answer to ask the next question)
Answer: Italy
Question: What type of person is an Italy-type of person?

Question: If I was a season, what season would I be?
(Let them answer and then use the answer to ask the next question)
Answer: Summer
Question: What type of person is a summer-type of person?

Once you have the answers then you can think them through and compare them with your own answers. Were you hard on yourself, or did you overplay your self image? Did your friends see something in you that you had never seen or thought of? Do you like the person you hear about, or would you prefer not to know him or her?

Remember, the analysis is meant to be light-hearted. If it turns out that everyone seems to see you in rather a negative light, then don't despair: you have recognised the fact, and now you can work on rectifying your image!

Here's an example of how this task might work. Sarah decided to ask a close friend what he thought about her. She decided to do it in the *Detox Your Mind* way.

Firstly she needed to ask the questions of herself:

If I was a car what make of car would I be?
A 2-seater jeep.

If I was a colour, what colour would I be?
Dark blue.

If I was a piece of fabric what kind of fabric would I be?
Denim.

Once the basic questions were answered she read her answers through and explained them. To Sarah a 2-seater jeep meant she was go-ahead, practical but quite light-hearted. Nothing was ever taken too seriously, but things got done because the car was functional and quick.

The colour dark blue meant that she felt herself to be cool but also a little mysterious – a bit of both worlds.

Denim is hard-wearing and versatile; Sarah thought that she resembled denim because she worked hard and could withstand pressure.

She thought that her answers had given her a pretty good description of herself: no fuss, no nonsense, practical, liked to get things done, with a sense of humour and a small element of mystery. She immediately called her friend and without any explanation, asked the same questions. The doubtless bewildered friend gave the following answers:

Car: MG sports car because they are fun and contemporary.

Colour: Orange because it is bright and vibrant.

Fabric: Crisp linen because it is practical yet stylish.

When Sarah analysed the answers and compared her friend's response with what she herself had said, she realised that there were several strong similarities. Her friend too saw her as a fun person, with a practical nature. However, he had attributed to her other qualities – brightness, vibrancy, stylishness – which she had not really realised she possessed. This gave her a massive boost of confidence in being herself; what was in her head was what other people saw. Her positive thoughts were giving off positive 'vibes'.

Important things to remember

Ask yourself the questions first.

Ask good friends or people who know you well.

Ask the questions without any prior warning and don't discuss their original answers.

Take a look at what they have said, compare it with what you have written and then decide if it is an accurate image of the real you.

Day 11

MAKE SOME ROOM IN YOUR HEAD

Today you are going to create some space in your head. Eliminate the negative and allow the positive to take its place.

We all have ghosts and skeletons in our minds. People who have done us wrong or harm; people who helped us but we never showed our gratitude; people who died without us telling them we loved them; people we hate because of something they did to someone we love; people we think are amazing but we've never let them know. We believe there is nothing we can do to change these thoughts, so we leave them there unchallenged, occupying valuable space that could be better used for something constructive.

Often it takes more courage or emotion than we are comfortable using to rectify a situation. Often it really is too late to be able to change a situation. But we still dwell on what might have been.

Today we can learn how to clean the thoughts away, or file them for future reference at a time when our circumstances may have changed.

The first step is to note down all the situations, with their attendant emotions, that:

- You constantly think about but know you cannot change

- You think you might be able to change but can't see a way of doing so

- You know you are able to change but haven't had the time/courage/inclination to do so

Now you can start to make amends for your neglect and clear your mind of its emotional clutter. Taking the situations one at a time, write a letter to them. Make sure that you discuss every issue that concerns you and describe exactly how you feel about the situation as it once was and as it now stands. Include your feelings about any repercussions or side-effects of the situation. Write down every single thought that comes into your mind, however unpleasant or even irrelevant it may seem. Today will not be an easy day – but it is worth the pain and the effort.

Once you have written your letter, read it through to yourself to make sure you have left nothing out. Then put it in an envelope and seal it. Address it to the person or situation it concerns (even if they have passed away).

You can now decide what to do with your letters – your unwanted emotional baggage. You may wish to put them in a safe place, under lock and key. If you prefer, you can destroy them. Wherever you put them, you can rest happy in the knowledge that the negativity they produced has been cleared from your mind. You have now said everything you ever wanted to say about a difficult situation – all those things you were never able to say face to face.

If you do decide to destroy the letters, it may be a wise idea to hold a small ceremony to put a final end to your negative thoughts by either burning the letters or shredding them into minute pieces. Burning letters full of love and words unsaid is symbolic; as the smoke rises, the words contained in the letters rise into the air also. You can tell yourself that they will reach the person they were meant for.

So: all your unsettled business is now settled. You have taken positive action. You have regained control and if you revisit those emotions in the future, you will do so from a calmer, more resolved perspective.

There is a lesson to be learned here. In future, if you have something to say, try to say it on the spot, so that it doesn't fester away for weeks or even years inside your head. If you don't want to say it in person, write it down and send it as a letter. The sooner you write, the more direct and the less bitter your words will be – the molehill won't have had time to become a mountain. But make sure that you think carefully before committing words to paper – once it has been sent, it has been said!

Day 12 _____

A CHANGE IS AS GOOD AS A REST

Inject some creativity into your life!

When was the last time you did something different on an everyday basis? When was the last time you changed your routine, either socially or at work? Every day we spend about 15 hours awake, yet every day we do the same thing.

Your routine gets you up at the same time each day. You have the same thing for breakfast. You go into your office, work until lunchtime, have lunch at your desk. You finish work at the same time every day. You get home, make a cup of coffee, watch TV, read the paper, go into the kitchen to make supper. Your partner gets in about an hour later and then you eat whilst watching TV until bed time. You sleep. Your partner gets up early to go to work, you say goodbye and then sleep for another hour. Then you get up, have the same thing for breakfast ...

There is no room in there for any imagination, any choice, any creativity. You know in advance what happens and when it happens, and so you have no need to think about changing anything. Now, if you were to change your routine, your mind would be required to act positively rather than operating on autopilot. To complete the same tasks within the same timeframe, you must keep your wits about you.

Your day of change should be all-encompassing; everything you normally do should be done differently. Choose a day that would have been completely run-of-the-mill and turn it upside down:

- Set the alarm earlier – or later
- Get out of the other side of the bed

- Have your shower/bath before breakfast, or after breakfast, whichever is not the norm

- Get dressed in a completely different outfit to that which you would normally choose. If you wear dark colours then opt for a bright colour, and vice versa. If you always wear suits, then wear separates; if you always wear trousers then wear a skirt; if you wear flat shoes then wear high heels

- If you wear make-up then go for the natural look. If you don't wear aftershave or perfume, put some on

- Get the bus instead of the car, or take the car instead of the train

- Use a carrier bag and not a briefcase

- Buy tea on the way into work rather than coffee

- Take the stairs to your office not the lift

- Make coffee for your secretary instead of letting him/her bring it to you

- If you normally buy a sandwich to eat at your desk, bring in a packed lunch

- If you normally call your friends in the afternoon, call them in the morning

- Leave later than normal – or earlier

- Catch a different train home. Choose a different route

- Cook something that you have never eaten before

- Read a book or listen to music instead of watching TV

- Do the ironing today instead of at the weekend

- Call your parents today instead of Friday

- Do the weekly shop late in the evening instead of on Saturday morning

- Read a book or talk about your day instead of going straight to sleep

Any of the above activities could make you look at your day completely differently. You will see things from a new perspective. Your stale routine will be invigorated and you may want to change it permanently or you may decide to go back to normal. Whichever you decide is fine; at least you have taken the opportunity to think about new ideas and question old ideas.

By changing your routine you will refresh your own life and send ripples out to everyone else. You will meet new people on the stairs; your colleagues will examine you in a new light, wondering why you are looking/acting differently. You may meet an old friend on the earlier train. Set the cat among the pigeons – give everyone something new to talk about and food for thought. Don't let them take you for granted!

Day 13

CHANGE AS A CATALYST
Doing something new means you learn something – and learning nourishes the mind.

Do something you have never done before and see how you like it and what you learn from it. There are lots of things that we just don't try, either because we are scared, because we consider them unsuitable or simply because we are stuck in a rut.

Today you must arrange, book or actually do 5 things that you have never before experienced. (There are floating days on which you can do some of these activities – you don't need to pack them all into one day!)

These things don't have to be expensive – the more expensive ones always have a less expensive alternative. If you want to try a food you have never previously tasted, cook it yourself, serve it up to friends and experience something new together. If you have never been to a football match then go to your local sports centre or read your local newspaper, find out where the local Sunday League teams play and turn up to support them – all free of charge. If you want to go to the opera or ballet then get a video out, dress up in your best clothes, dim the lights and hey presto – the Royal Opera in your own home!

It may be something very simple that you have never tried – I know of someone who has never eaten pasta or yogurt! – but whatever it is, it must be an entirely new experience for you.

Here are a few suggestions:

- Go to a play
- Watch a rugby match
- Eat frogs' legs
- Eat shark steaks
- Go to an aquarium
- Go to a safari park
- Make a cake

- Cook an exotic meal

- Read a play

- Go for a jog

Once you have done your 'new' things you should think about how they made you feel. Encourage everyone you know to try something new themselves. This makes your new experience have an effect on lots more people than just you – it's those ripples-in-a-pond again.

If you share something new with your friends they may tell you about something new they have done. And before you know it your horizons have been expanded tremendously and you know far more than you did before you started on this journey of discovery.

Day 14

GET SOME THERAPY
Today you should book a treatment of your choice – anything so long as it will clear your mind and help you relax both physically and, more importantly, mentally. Listed below are some of the more mentally stimulating treatments that you could try during your programme to lift your mind and energise your spirits.

Acupuncture
Acupuncture is based on Traditional Chinese Medicine. The basis of Traditional Chinese Medicine is that the body

operates on a series of meridians, which relate to every point in the body and facilitate the flow of 'Chi' or 'energy' within the body. If there is an illness or problem within a person, this results in a blockage at some point along the meridians, causing an imbalance. Acupuncture aims to clear any blockages, thus bringing the body back into balance, with optimum energy flow.

Your first treatment will consist of an in-depth case history taken by your practitioner. You may find that some of the questions are a little unusual; the acupuncturist will be trying to discover what in your life may have caused an imbalance. The practitioner is likely to start the 'hands-on' treatment by taking your pulses; there are six on each wrist and these will give an indication of what is happening inside your body. They may also look at your tongue as this is a window to your body. The needles are the next part of the treatment; they are not as painful as many people assume. The needles we are used to in Western medicine are used to inject fluid into our bodies; the needle must be much thicker to allow the fluid to pass through. Acupuncture needles are incredibly fine. As they are inserted into the flesh you are likely to feel some sensation, but very little or no pain. The needles are left in place for a short period of time and then removed.

Acupuncture is often used in specific cases of pain or illness: period problems, back pain, liver/kidney complaints, blood pressure, circulatory problems etc. Acupuncturists also use the treatment to alleviate psychological conditions such as stress, anxiety, depression and exhaustion. Acupuncture is one of the complementary therapies that is more widely recognised by general practitioners and it is widely accepted as a therapy.

Aromatherapy

Aromatherapy is the name given to the use of plant-extracted essential oils. Many people believe that aromatherapy is simply 'a nice-smelling massage'; but it is much, much more than this. Essential oils are absorbed into our bodies via the skin or the olfactory system (inhalation). The skin is a semi-permeable membrane and the transfer of the essential oil molecules through the skin into the bloodstream means that the effects can begin as soon as the oils are applied to the skin. They will continue as long as the oils are on the surface of the flesh. Once in the bloodstream the molecules will travel to the brain and trigger the necessary functions relevant to the specific oil used. (Initial doubt as to whether substances can be absorbed through the skin has been eliminated by the introduction of 'patches' for many conditions by the medical industry.)

If we inhale the essential oil fragrance then the molecules travel inside the nostril and reach the brain through the thin membranes in the nasal passage and the olfactory system. Inhaling the oils is the quickest way to benefit from them as this is the quickest way to absorb oils into the system (sniffing drugs or illegal substances has always been the fastest way to experience their effects).

There are many stimulating and uplifting oils available, as well as some more specific oils to clear the mind of negative feelings. Oils can also be used to boost the body's immune system, so that during times of overwork or exhaustion they can protect you.

There is a lengthier description of oils and their benefits in the third section of this book. I would recommend an aromatherapy massage for this stage of the programme as it is a thoroughly relaxing treatment. The practitioner will put you at ease and you can focus on yourself throughout the treatment, concentrating on thinking calm and positive thoughts.

Essential oils should never be used if you believe you are pregnant or if you are trying to become pregnant unless otherwise prescribed by a trained aromatherapist. Essential oils should never be taken internally.

Bach Flower Remedies

Bach flower remedies can be bought from any larger chemist; the instructions on how to use each remedy will be enclosed. Alternatively you can get blends mixed by a local practitioner for use at different times of the day/month/year – or whenever they are required.

Bach flower remedies are extremely useful during your Detox Programme as they address mental or emotional anguish, leaving a clear mind, uncluttered by negative thoughts or feelings.

Bach flower remedies were introduced to the world by Dr Edward Bach. He believed that any illness we suffer is derived from a mental imbalance. Dr Bach used his flower remedies to treat problems based on the emotional state of the patient; he would look at their personality, moods and temperament and then prescribe accordingly. He aimed to heal the mind in order to heal the body. This holistic approach is often adopted in modern-day medicine when we discuss illnesses that are 'stress-related' or 'tension-induced'.

The remedies are extracted from the flowers, plants or bark by soaking them in fresh water. The water is then preserved in brandy and taken as and when you need it. Bach remedies are taken by placing a small amount of the remedy – one single drop – on the tongue until the feelings have subsided. You can build your own personal 'kit' for every emotional state you may find yourself experiencing.

If you want to use flower remedies you are unlikely to find a practitioner that deals solely with the Bach remedies; they are usually used as an adjunct to another therapy. Use this day to find a practitioner who will combine flower remedies with something else that will make you feel good and concentrate your mind.

There are 38 Bach remedies and these are further divided into seven groups, or emotional states. This makes them an excellent addition to your Detox programme. They can be used in a combination or blend, or on their own:

Fear	Terror
	Fear of known things
	Fear of mind giving way
	Fears or worries of unknown origin
	Fear or over-concern for others
Uncertainty	Seeks advice and confirmation from others Indecision
	Discouragement and despondency
	Hopelessness and despair
	Monday-morning feeling
	Uncertainty as to the correct path in life
Insufficient interest in current circumstances	Dreaminess, lack of interest in present
	Lives in the past
	Resignation, apathy
	Lack of energy
	Unwanted thoughts, mental arguments
	Deep gloom with no origin
	Failure to learn from past mistakes

Loneliness	Proud, aloof
	Impatience
	Self-centeredness, self-concern
Oversensitivity to influence and ideas	Mental torment behind a brave face
	Weak-willed and subservient
	Protection from change and outside influence
	Hatred, envy and jealousy
Despondency or despair	Lack of confidence
	Self-reproach, guilt
	Overwhelmed by responsibility
	Extreme mental anguish
	After-effects of shock
	Resentment
	Exhausted but struggles on
	Self-hatred, sense of uncleanness
Over-care for welfare of others	Selfishly possessive
	Over-enthusiasm
	Domineering, inflexible
	Intolerance
	Self-repression, self-denial

Colonic Irrigation

Colonic irrigation has been around since as early as 1500BC, but it seems to be a relatively new and experimental therapy for most people in the 20th century.

Colonic irrigation is an internal bath that helps to cleanse the colon of accumulated poisons, gases, faecal matter and mucous deposits. The practitioner will gently pump filtered water into the rectum and this will start to soften and flush away any unwanted build-up of toxins and waste.

Colonic irrigation is extremely effective during the Detox programme. Colonics are reported to leave the patient with a feeling of euphoria and clear thinking – confirming the statement 'A healthy body means a healthy mind'.

Colonics is not something that normally springs to mind as a mind-clearing therapy. But many people claim that colonics leaves them with a totally clear head, and book regular treatments to balance mind and body. If you have ever thought about trying this treatment to see what the effects would be, then today is the time to go for it! It's painless, it's different, it makes you feel great and it is detox-ifying – physically and mentally.

The colonics practitioner will ask you to lie on a couch or plinth, with your lower body covered with a towel or sheet. Filtered water at a carefully regulated temperature is introduced under gentle gravitational pressure through the rectum and into the colon. The practitioner will use massage to help the water soften and cleanse the colon of faecal matter and waste that is flushed away with the waste water. The colon is worked on in stages; each time water is pumped in and flushed out until the whole process is complete. The treatment will last less than an hour and the modesty of the client is observed throughout the treatment – practitioners are totally aware of the 'unusual' circum-stances that they place their clients in. It is usual for the practitioner to recommend how many further treatments are required and also which supplements to replace natural bowel fibre and flora are needed.

Cranio-Sacral Therapy

Cranio-sacral therapy is the ultimate treatment if you like the idea of being held whilst feeling your body's ills and tensions float away as you become 'balanced' one more. By very subtly working the cranium, spine and sacrum, the treatment releases any tensions that have built up and returns your body to its natural flow.

Cranio-sacral therapy can be used for all head, neck and shoulder tensions but can also work on very deep-seated tensions and problems that the mind has held on to for many years. Treatments can be a physical and emotional release and can have some quite profound effects.

Indian Head Massage

Indian head massage has been practised in India for over a thousand years. Originally women used the technique to keep their long hair in a healthy and beautiful condition – they still do this today.

Massage has the effect of nourishing the hair roots and prevents excessive hair loss. For both men and women, old and young, it can be an extremely relaxing treatment and when combined with neck and shoulder treatments it will leave the client 'floating'. Indian head massage relaxes the scalp, tones up the subcutaneous muscles and helps to reduce headaches and eyestrain.

Our bad posture habits mean that a series of Indian head treatments help to release tensions built up in the neck and shoulder area whilst also stimulating blood flow to the grey matter!

Flotation

Flotation tanks use saline solution to create the ultimate feeling of floating. The water is blood-temperature; there is no light, no sound (or just a simple relaxation tape playing in the background); you are also weightless, as the saline solution totally supports your body.

After relaxing into your own breathing pattern, the only thing you are aware of is you and what is going on inside you. Flotation deprives you of all normal outside sensations; your muscles relax completely as they no longer need to bear your weight. Flotation is a great help in cases of stress and stress-related tension. If you manage to totally relax and truly 'float', then you feel reborn as all of life's problems simply disappear. Your mind is cleared of all outside stimulus so you can concentrate on yourself, spend time with an empty head, released from any need for thought.

Light Therapy

Seasonal Affective Disorder (SAD) is an illness that has been identified in recent years and light therapy is one of the ways in which it can be treated. Our bodies operate in normal daylight conditions – certain amounts of light and darkness in any 24-hour period. It is when these hours are adjusted during winter that some people develop emotional and hormonal imbalances. Everyone knows just how exhilarating and uplifting a sunny day can be – and, conversely, how dreary a dull day can be. For many people this feeling goes a lot deeper and can actually become a major cause of depression, lethargy and apathy.

Light therapy exposes the patient to periods of strong white light which help to restore hormonal balance. The light also causes the body to produce essential Vitamin B (needed for energy). Once a course of treatment has been completed the effects can be seen to be very beneficial.

Yoga

Yoga used to be the only 'complementary therapy' that anyone had ever heard of. It wasn't even classed as alternative – it was the sort of thing your mother went to one night a week in order to get out of the house and away from the children! Yoga nowadays has come into its own. It can be intensely meditative or it can be very physically demanding, – almost gymnastic – so choose your class carefully.

Whatever the type of yoga you practise you will definitely feel invigorated and refreshed after your class. The beauty of yoga lies with its ability to teach calm and serenity. There is something very balletic about yoga and you will feel graceful and balanced after even a short session.

The calm and serenity it brings will help you deal, through breathing and relaxation exercises, with many of life's problems. See the third section for further information on yoga and what it can do to detox your mind.

Metamorphic Technique

Metamorphic technique is quite a hard treatment to explain, probably because it is not classed as a treatment and many practitioners do not class themselves as practitioners. They would be better described as facilitators and the client as receivers.

The metamorphic technique works on the principle that our feet are a canvas for the way we spent our time in the womb. Anything that happened in development is laid out on our feet: our manner, our characteristics, our personality. Simply by touching the feet in certain places, metamorphic technique can serve to free our life force. The life force is released by the facilitator concentrating and focusing on the client, who can then go on to use the force to benefit their bodies and minds.

Metamorphic technique seems to be particularly helpful for people suffering from addictions, or illnesses that cause loss of self-esteem or generate self-doubt and weaknesses: ME, alcohol and drug addiction, anorexia. Metamorphic technique also seems to help those with long-term mental and physical illness or problems.

The treatment will take about an hour. All of this time is spent 'allowing' the body to heal itself. The practitioner will make a series of stroking or holding motions – sometimes without physically touching the body. The treatment is designed to build the self-esteem and confidence of the client. There is no hard and fast rule about how many treatments you should have; this decision can only be made by the client themselves, as only they know how they are feeling.

Day 15

MAKE THEIR DAY – AND YOURS
Paying a compliment means that you will have given someone something positive and brightened their day – which in turn will make you feel positive.

Today, you must pay a compliment to a friend and a stranger – adapting the nature of your compliment according to the recipient. As with the smiling, this will only work if the compliment is genuine. You will need to be very observant and give careful thought to everyone you see.

Look at people and focus on the positive things about them. Try to think about one good thing to say about everyone you meet. You will find that this lifts your spirits and makes the world a much nicer place to be. If you think it's appropriate (and, in the case of a stranger, if you think the compliment will be well received), pass your positive comment on. Tell people that they are 'wearing a colour that really suits them'; or that they 'have a lovely jumper on'; or 'always cheer you up'. If so much is right with the world, not a lot can be wrong, can it?

You don't have to pay your compliments in person. Say something positive to everyone you speak to on the phone; or fax; or e-mail. Try and put yourself in the position of the person with whom you are communicating. Imagine how their day is going, how they are feeling right now. What would make you feel good, if you were in their shoes? If they sound down in the dumps, congratulate them on the recent report they wrote, or let them know that they called at exactly the right time because you'd been thinking of them; or tell them it would be great to get together as you'd value their opinion on something. Although you can't be as personal as you could be face to face, you can give them a positive boost.

Go ahead – make someone's day.

Day 16

POSITIVE THINKING

This Detox programme is about positive thinking as a way of life. Positive thinking is cleansing for the mind because positive energy is healthy and vital. Now is your chance to use it.

Today you must have the most positive day of your life. Positive thinking is sometimes hard, but it is always rewarding.

The frame of mind you are in can totally dictate your day. It will determine if you have a great time – or if you wish you never got out of bed. Being in a positive frame of mind lets you do anything you want to; being in a negative state of mind can prevent you from attempting the most menial of tasks – you just can't summon up the interest or enthusiasm.

Good news is 'wonderful' if you are in a positive mood; and good news is 'about the only thing that has gone right' if you are in a bad mood. Positive thinking puts problems into context. It clears the mind to tackle the present moment with joy and ingenuity.

Positive thinking is hard work, however. It is much more easy to think negatively. The main reason for this is that we learn from the world around us to think negatively. We are encouraged to be cynical and sceptical by nature, refusing to trust people in case they might try to deceive us for their own ends. We expect people to earn our trust – they are guilty until proved innocent. We believe that everyone has a personal agenda which means they are always out to 'get something' – and something for nothing at that. We try and protect ourselves by being instinctively suspicious of anything new. The fear of the unknown makes us negative towards change. Positive thinking does not mean throwing caution to the wind and being reckless – but it does mean keeping an open mind.

Important things to remember

Talk yourself through every action or observation and add a positive thought or comment to each.

Add a positive comment to each verbal observation or comment you make.

If you think a negative thought or make a negative comment, then turn it into a positive by adding something nice to the sentence or thought.

Keep checking that you are doing it – you may forget and let a few hours pass without doing any positive thinking.

Once you get into the habit you become aware of two things: firstly, just how easy it is to be negative about the smallest thing that really isn't a problem if you stop to think; and, secondly that positive thinking makes life so much easier and more pleasant for everyone you meet, as well as for yourself.

Day 17

DREAMS AND WISHES

Today you have permission to daydream about anything you want to!

This will totally release you from the real world with its stresses and limitations. You can wish for anything you want to. When you get more used to indulging dreams and wishes you will be able to go off on these empowering flights of fancy whenever you want – but as a beginner it's best to set aside a specific time.

You must, of course, have real fun while you're doing it. As with everything on this programme, your dreams can be as personal or selfish as you want – but they must be things which you have already dreamed about. Anything goes. The sky's the limit!

- I want to fly to the moon
- I want to invent a new product that changes the world
- I wish I had a Prince Charming
- I want to sing live to an audience of at least 10,000 people
- I want to go on safari
- I want to rule the world

Once you have made your wish-list then sit back and give yourself up to it. Imagine yourself ruling the world; on safari with the partner of your dreams by your side; with tickets to the moon in your back pocket; with the smell of the grease-paint and roar of the crowd still fresh in your mind from last night's concert; waiting to hear from the patent department about your world-beating supermarket trolley that always goes in the direction in which you actually push it! Feels good, doesn't it? And I bet you have at least a smile on your face by now, if you haven't actually laughed out loud.

In your mind you can be and do anything you want to – so go ahead! Dream on and wish away.

Now that you have got into the swing of it you can get on with your normal day, yet transform it into the most amazing day you have ever had: a day-dream. Everything you do today will be the stuff that dreams are made of. Leave your house and shut the door on your mansion in the South of France. Walk along the road to the bus stop because you need to leave the £70,000 sports car behind once in a while to have it hand-polished by the 18-year-old drop-dead-gorgeous pool boy – he should do something for his money! Get to work quickly to see how your multi-million-pound organic vegetable company is doing. Give everybody a 50% pay rise because profit figures show that you are doing very well indeed. When you have picked the children up from school you will all be going to see Mickey Mouse who has called to say that he has a spare hour or so and can he come and entertain the children whilst you prepare a sumptuous feast for Leonardo DiCaprio? After having the meal the children say they want to go to bed as they are tired and you and Leonardo fly off to the coast to see the sun set. Once you return you can go to bed – to awake to a breakfast of fresh fruit salad with lightly poached eggs on golden toast ... I think you get the picture.

You see, you can have everything and anything you want, every day of you life. Just dream for a few minutes – it doesn't cost a penny and it feels so good. What's more, you've exercised your imagination and helped yourself establish what you want from life.

'Dreamers' and 'people who wish their life away', are always criticised: as if they have no real ambitions, or cannot come to terms with what is real. But if you *know* that you are dreaming or wishing and you are happy to return to the real world revitalised, happy and refreshed, having had a little entertainment and excitement, then you have an advantage over your less imaginative colleagues. For you are fully aware, not only of the outer, 'real' world, but of your own inner world – the world of your mind.

And if you don't have dreams they can never come true!

Day 18

LEARN 5 NEW THINGS

Today you will learn 5 new things, crank up the grey matter

and give your mind a work-out. These things must be useful to you on a day-to-day basis. They should be things that you use regularly but which you have to source every time you use them as they have not been committed to memory. By the end of the day you will have saved yourself time, improved your memory and exercised your brain!

You might choose:

- Telephone numbers of family and friends

- PIN numbers of bank cards or credit cards

- Addresses of friends and family

- Birthdays

- Ages of friends/relatives

- Dates of the annual Bank Holidays

- Security code to your suitcase lock

- Detailed directions to your house from the nearest motorway

When you have chosen your list, write it down clearly on a piece of card or paper that you can carry with you all day. Read it at every opportunity and recite it in your head whenever you are walking, travelling, queuing or not thinking about anything specific.

Get friends to test you. Make sure that you commit as much to memory as possible before you go to bed at night. You should keep the list to test yourself during the next few days. Recite the list whenever you can: first thing in the morning as you clean your teeth; whilst you wait for the kettle to boil; while you are waiting for the next tube/bus to arrive.

Learning something by rote means you are finding out exactly how your memory works. Do you learn better given small nuggets of information, or is it easier to recite a whole list in a certain rhythm, like a poem? Do you use shorthand to learn i.e. by making up a short story that includes all the relevant information, or do you simply learn the list in its entirety?

Try to use the information you have learned as soon as possible. Write to your friends, phone your family, check your bank balance by punching in the PIN, ask your nephew how it feels now that he is Xyrs old (don't forget the half/quarter year – very important when you are only 6!)

If you already have all these things committed to memory, then well done. But you don't get let off the task. If you truly have nothing practical to learn then you must choose a poem or paragraph from a book or play and learn this. Choose 5 lines and follow the same instructions as above. Choose your piece carefully because, just as you will need to use the addresses and phone numbers, you must use the paragraph in conversation as soon as possible – it should therefore be appropriate.

There! Who said you cannot teach an old dog new tricks? You have just saved yourself a lot of time and effort by committing information to memory and given yourself a 'mental workout' in the process.

Day 19

YOUR 5-YEAR PLAN

You are now more than half-way through this Detox Programme and you know a lot more about what you really think and want than you did at the beginning. It is now time to make some plans – 5-year plans.

Most of the time we just get on with life. We don't *live* it or experience it. That seems to be what life is all about – getting through what we have to do every day, getting up when we are tired, getting breakfast for ourselves, the children, getting them to school, getting dressed, getting to work, getting through work, getting the children from school, getting the dinner, getting things ready for the next day ...

If we never stop to think about where we are really going, what we actually want rather than what everybody wants from us, then life can really get the better of us. Day-to-day living is unavoidable, but without our own personal plan it may be all we have. We will never be able to move forwards.

Making your plan is not difficult. Simply sit down with a cup of tea/coffee and write about what you really want out of life. What you *Really* want. Not what, in defeat or apathy, you are prepared to accept. Your life plan should be based in reality, but there is plenty of scope for dreams and wishes – and they are equally important. Never give up on your dreams and wishes (you should be an expert at dreams and wishes by now!) But try to focus on what you *know* – because you now know yourself – is achievable.

Every time you have a few seconds to yourself you can turn your personal tiller a fraction further in the direction of your plan. Slowly but surely you will achieve your goals if you know what they are. If you don't, then you will simply drift and stumble through life, letting things happen to you rather than making them happen.

Your 5-year plan is not set in stone. You are entitled to change your aims and goals at any time. Nor is it an opportunity for you to fulfil all those dreams which mothers, fathers, teachers always had for you. Your plan should allow you to achieve what is important for you personally. No one else need ever know what it is that you crave. You can be brutally honest, or brutally selfish. This is all about *you* – and you cannot possibly be important to anyone else unless you are important to yourself.

Some of the goals in your 5-year plan might read like this:

- Get through the next six months without going completely mad

- Find a new job closer to home within the next year

- Increase my earnings by 15% within the next five years

- Go on a three-week holiday without taking any of my in-laws

- Decorate the lounge by Christmas

- Spend at least half an hour a day in conversation with my partner

Some of these goals are very modest and based on the short-term; some will require a little more thought and are based on the long-term. But all are equally important. If you manage to get the new job but fail to decorate the lounge, you will not be completely satisfied with your life. If you manage the conversation each day you may survive the next six months without going mad!

Remember: this plan is yours and yours only. It is based on your needs. And the progress you make towards the goals it lists should be measurable. It's far better to be realistic and aim towards what you know is feasible. Setting yourself a goal of a 15% salary increase within 5 years is much more feasible

– and achievable – than planning to be a millionaire. But don't be too unambitious. And remember that some of your goals will have in-built rewards that you never expected. If you change jobs in order to be nearer home, for example, your new job will bring with it a whole new range of opportunities. If you go on holiday without your in-laws, you will return so inspired and invigorated that you will be in a much better position to get that promotion you want. As you start making the little things come true, the big things are much more likely to follow suit!

Day 20

SILENCE IS GOLDEN

You have completed your 5-year plan. Now it is time for contemplation, so you are ready to start fulfilling that plan.

Today should be a day off work, a weekend or a holiday as you will spend it in total silence! If it doesn't fall on a convenient day, then do a swap with another 'task' so that it does.

Getting to know what is really in your head is much easier if you are not interacting with anyone. If the only dialogue you have all day is with yourself, then you can find out a lot about yourself. It is like being locked in a room with one person, free to ask any question you wish. The experience may be quite intense, but you will get answers to the questions.

There are many places that call themselves 'retreats', places where people can go to stay for a time of reflection or prayer. You do not enter into conversation with anyone while on retreat, so you can focus 100% on your reasons for being there. You can re-create a retreat in your own home. Spend your time thinking for yourself; writing lists, writing letters; exploring problems, dilemmas and ideas without being influenced by others.

You will need to prepare for this day by shutting yourself off from the outside world and outside stimuli. Put the answerphone on or unplug the phone. Lock the front door and do not answer it. Do not open the post. Ban radio, television, videos, newspapers and books from your home. Make sure the day takes up a full 24 hours, from, say, 11pm the night before until 11pm on the day of your retreat. If you use your retreat day to catch up on lost sleep, then that is very useful. That is what you personally need to do to recharge your batteries.

You should dress in something loose, warm and comfortable. If you need to sleep, then sleep until you wake. Don't be regulated by clocks. You can go back to bed for rest as and when required during the day. For the rest of your retreat time you should avoid everyday activity. Don't try to do the household chores, tidy the house. You are on retreat in order to escape from all these pressures. Being on retreat should mean you can 'touch base' with yourself – maybe for the first time ever.

You may discover that it is the first time for ages that you have spent 24 hours entirely alone, away from the demands of your usual daily routine. Use the day to answer any questions you have in your mind. If you have any problems with relationships, then use the time to think through all your options. If you need to decide about a career change, then think this through carefully and at length. The fact that you cannot communicate with the outside world means that, if you reach a decision, you will have to live with it for several hours before you tell anyone. This will give you more time to reflect and to confirm if the decision is right or wrong for you. If there is a lot going on in your life then your day of silence may simply serve to 'let you unwind' before you carry on with business as usual.

If you believe that you are already very organised and that there is nothing you need time to think about, then well done – what's your secret?! But you should still 'retreat'. Use the time for relaxation exercises, correct breathing and doing nothing. Doing nothing is harder than it sounds! Listen to your breathing; feel your heartbeat; become aware of every aspect of your mind and body. When you feel they are in total harmony then you should prepare a simple meal from the Brain Food section and get an early night. You may find that after such deep, thorough relaxation your dreams are very much more vivid; your mind has been cleared of all the anxieties and stresses that usually muddy your subconscious.

Important things to remember

Remove outside stimuli from the place of your retreat – no phones, faxes, post, television, radio, newspapers or books. And no people.

If the views from your retreat show the world going on as usual, then don't look out of the window.

Focus on your own innermost thoughts.

Awake feeling refreshed and invigorated and armed with the clear-headed thinking that your day of silence created.

Day 21

BACK TO BASICS

Today is about getting back to basics. You will discover that you can have fun and entertainment without a lot of thought and effort. Open your mind and have a good time!

Relaxation and enjoyment is the order of the day today. We are going to take a trip down Memory Lane and hunt for all the games you played as a young child.

Tiddlywinks; Monopoly; Snakes and Ladders; Snap; Draughts; Cluedo; Mousetrap; Kerplunk, Hangman, Twister; Dot to Dot; Beetle Drive; Noughts and Crosses; the list goes on, depending on how old you are.

You will relax as you rediscover the familiar domain of childhood games. You will also recover memories of how you felt when you played them for the first time. When life was simple; when you didn't need to present a protective façade to the world; when you had no cares or responsibilities.

You will certainly need to use your brain. Deciding whether or not to invest in a hotel on Park Lane, or whether it was Colonel Mustard in the library with the candlestick, may not challenge you, but will still exercise parts of your mind that you don't always use on a day-to-day basis. Thinking for entertainment; being cunning for fun; and planning for notional victory are all uplifting and very invigorating.

Laughter should play a major part in your life today. You are unlikely to want to play games *all* day; today would be a good day to invite friends around after work. You can fulfil your task by asking them to participate in 'The Tiddlywinks Championship – First Round'. This activity need not interfere with your normal routine; unless, of course, you decide to take one day of your annual holiday entitlement in order to limber up and surprise the unsuspecting competition ...

Relaxation and light-hearted socialising puts the toils and difficulties of the day into perspective. Problems can be made more bearable by spending time with friends, having a good laugh. Laughter releases hormones that make you feel good – it is very true that laughter is the best tonic.

When you go to bed at the end of the day, look back and ask yourself if you enjoyed the games and why. Was it because you won? Was it because a friend was surprisingly enthusiastic? Was it because it made a really nice and unexpected end to the day? Or was it because you hadn't done anything like that for ages?

Whatever your reasons, you have abandoned yourself to a wholly simple pleasure. You have cast off, albeit for only a few hours, the mantle of adult problems and woes. You have looked at life from a new perspective. Without using too much brain power, you have upped your personal feelgood factor. Hold on to that thought as you fall asleep. And try not to smile too broadly in tomorrow's meeting as you retrieve a mental picture of your normally sedate and unbending colleague desperately trying to get the final leg into his bright green Beetle before its antennae fall out for the tenth time ...

Day 22

FLOATING DAY

Use today to catch up with incomplete tasks – or do something different from Day 13.

Phew!

Day 23

BRAIN BOOSTERS

If you ever need a boost to energise your mind, or a calming influence so that you can concentrate, then the 5 tools from Day 23 will set you up for life. Cleansing, boosting, clarifying and energising, these tools can go with you wherever you are and can provide instant results.

Carrying a 'kick-start' kit with you in your bag or briefcase wherever you go can be a real advantage. You will need:

- Menthol/peppermint chewing gum, extra strong mints or herbal sweets

- Basil, grapefruit and lemon essential oils

- A small dark glass bottle with watertight top and dropper – health food shops or chemists stock these

- 100mls of carrier oil – olive, sunflower, grapeseed or almond

Self head-and-face massage – 5-minute pick-you-up for instant energy

The following sequence can be learnt in a matter of moments and will give you an extra few hours' energy – at no cost:

1. Place elbows on a table top in front of you and cup hands together.

2. Gently lower head into your hands with eyes closed and rest to the count of 10 – count out loud, but quietly.

3. Concentrate on breathing through your belly and exhaling every last bit of air before you inhale again.

4. Keep relaxing your shoulders.

5. Spread fingers so that your head is resting on the tips. Slowly rotate your fingers into your scalp – you should be moving the flesh across your scalp, not your fingers across the flesh. Move your fingers to cover the entire scalp and neck area.

6. Place thumbs on temples whilst your head is still resting in your hands. Slowly apply equal pressure to temples and when it is as firm as it feels comfortable, hold and rotate ends of fingers into temples – not over the flesh but pushing into the flesh. Release the pressure slowly and repeat.

7. Place thumbs either side of the bridge of your nose, just at the top of the inner eye socket. Lower weight of head onto thumbs. Hold until tension eases away and release.

8. Sit upright with your head no longer resting on your hands and push your fingers into your hair as if 'tearing your hair out'. Gently grab handfuls of the hair – at the root, as this will stop any pulling – and firmly lift the roots away from the scalp as if you are trying to let extra blood flow between skin and scalp. (This is exactly what you are doing.)

9. Release the 'pull' and move hands to another area and repeat until the whole scalp has been covered.

10. Sit upright, pull shoulders down and then slowly lower your head down to the left shoulder, hold the stretch and then lower to the right shoulder. Keep looking directly ahead, do not twist your neck.

11. Shrug your shoulders up as tightly as you can and release – repeat 4 times.

You should now be completely revived and ready for anything the day has to offer.

Essential oils for mental fatigue

Make a blend of 10 drops each of basil, lemon and grapefruit essential oils and carry this round with you in a small bottle. If you need a pick-you-up to 'cure' brain burn-out or mental fatigue then simply add a few drops of the blend to your burner (see Aromatherapy section of book). As you inhale the airborne fragrance, feel your brain wake up and revive.

Mix some drops in a carrier oil and take a long bath at body temperature; remember to inhale deeply during your bath.

Mix some of the blend with a base body oil and rub into pressure points on the wrists and temples.

Alternatively you can place the bottle a couple of feet away from you on your desk or work surface and as the fragrance reaches you inhale deeply – do not inhale directly from the bottle as the aroma is far too concentrated and may cause headaches. (NB: always test your skin for any reaction on a small area before applying blends containing essential oils directly to your body.)

These oils will have an immediate effect and you do not need to use much. They should be mixed in a dark bottle and kept out of sunlight. When using the oils for bathing add a maximum of 10 drops to a tablespoon of carrier oil before adding to a bath. Add 5 or 6 drops of the blend to a burner. When using as a massage oil you should add 10 drops of the essential oil blend per 100mls of carrier oil.

Deep breathing

Your balance and alertness of mind are affected by your breathing. If you are tense and stressed, your breathing will be short and shallow and you will be less likely to be able to think straight. A short exercise in deep breathing should bring your energy back and your mind into focus.

To breathe correctly simply relax your stomach muscles, inhale through your nose slowly and take in air until it feels like the base of your stomach is full of air. Pause momentarily and then exhale through the mouth. By feeling the air 'in your stomach' it shows that you have relaxed your diaphragm muscle, which means your lungs have fully expanded and you have inhaled to full capacity. This will feel strange at first, but it will soon become the normal way to breathe.

40 winks

Taking a nap in the middle of the day or whenever you are so tired you simply cannot concentrate any more can be all that is needed to relax and refresh your mind. If you feel you cannot focus on the task in hand, go to a quiet place, or just rest your head on your arms on your desk, and take 10 minutes' relaxation time. You may actually fall asleep; or you may just close your eyes. But after that 10 minutes you will feel energised and fully revitalised.

Menthol Air

Chewing a menthol sweet or gum can give a simulated 'fresh air' injection. Practise your breathing techniques while chewing and the strong menthol/peppermint or eucalyptus will shock your brain into action. If you have access to fresh mint or eucalyptus leaves, crush a few leaves in your palms and inhale the stimulating fragrance.

Day 24

SELF-ESTEEM

Clear your mind of negative thoughts or doubts about yourself and your capabilities.

If you believe in yourself and have self-respect and self-esteem then life is much more pleasurable. Problems are easy to solve; you can turn your hand to anything; you feel good about yourself. You can do, think, be anything if you have positive self-esteem. Today is about getting yourself some self-esteem, boosting what esteem you already have and affirming that you are, quite simply, uniquely brilliant!

If people try to criticise you or demoralise you, then self-esteem will put their negativity into perspective. Without self-esteem, doubts and worries can assume large proportions, for no other reason except your own lack of belief in yourself. If you are not quite sure of your own abilities, a little self-esteem will make you sure. If you are put in a position where you no longer have the support of others, self-esteem will help you find a way to stand alone and make things work for you.

Self-esteem is essential. It makes you feel confident. It gives you the strength to believe wholeheartedly in your own powers.

The perfect person does not exist. Therefore no one else is better than you. We all have faults, imperfections, weaknesses. Keep telling yourself that you have no more than the next person. Accentuate the positive – dwell on your good points to convince yourself of your worth. And remember that you are important. To you, you are the most important person in the world! If you are insecure about your value

Today we are going to increase your general awareness of the world about you, which will in turn heighten your imaginative powers. For example, what do you really look like? You look in the mirror every morning when you clean your teeth or make up your face – but could you draw your face if you had to? You go to your office every day – but could you describe it in minute detail if asked?

What colour is your neighbour's front door?

What colour is your neighbour's car?

What is your local corner shop actually called?

What shape are the chairs in your favourite restaurant?

What does a £10 note look like?

How many shops do you pass on the way to the post office?

What does the pharmacist in your local chemist look like?

Today you must 'draw' at least three of the items from the above list, including all the information you can remember about that person or thing. This exercise is like a personal *Police File* – describe everything as if you were giving evidence. What characteristics does the person or thing have that make it unique?

Once you have completed your descriptions, go out and see how closely your version of events compares with the reality. Were you miles out – suggesting you are pretty unobservant – or does your description serve a useful purpose? Think about how often you have *seen* the thing you described before – but never actually *looked*.

In the future, try to keep your eyes open and your wits about you as you move around. Open your mind to what is out there. You will be amazed how much more you can see in everyday situations – often the commonplace will become something quite inspiring or beautiful. Search out the positive, the fascinating, the unusual – the things that give you a buzz and make you feel good. Analyse what you see. What has made that face so serious? Why has your neighbour chosen to paint their lounge walls that colour? (It won't be just lack of taste!) Let your imagination run wild and invent a fantasy which might explain the reality.

Open your mind to the everyday and the ordinary – and make it unusual and extraordinary.

Day 26

AFFIRMATIONS AND VISUALISATIONS

Today you will learn how to create your own affirmations and carry out your own visualisations. These will empower you to deal with any situation that occurs in the future. They will help you handle difficult and stressful situations and give you tremendous confidence.

Affirmations and visualisation are a brilliant way of feeling good about yourself immediately, with long-term benefits as well. Feeling down in the dumps can be transformed into feeling positive and proactive in a matter of moments; and when you have got into the habit of affirming and visualising, feeling stressed or fearful becomes a thing of the past.

If someone tells you something often enough, you start to believe it. That's how affirmations and visualisations work.

If you tell yourself something – anything – often enough, it will become true.

Affirmations

To start making affirmations you need to think about what your goal is. What specifically do you want the affirmation to help you make happen? It can be on any level: job, home, relationship, money – anything. It is probably better to start with something easily achievable. Going to live on a tropical island might be a little too ambitious for starters! And remember: if you change the small things, the big things come within your reach.

Affirmations must be positive and brief. The sorts of things you may want to affirm could be:

- My mind is relaxed

- My thoughts are clear

- I can deal with anything the day throws at me

- I love a challenge

- My nerves are a sign that my body is prepared

- I am feeling great

- I am feeling energetic

- I will succeed

- I deserve more money

- I will assert myself

Now all you have to do is repeat them, to yourself or out loud. You should say them whenever they come into your mind; you should say them whenever you are beset by doubts or anxieties. As you are saying your affirmations you should empower them with positive energy. Feel good about saying them; smile whilst you are saying them. Believe that they can come true or are coming true for you. If, after saying your affirmations, you still feel negative, then say them again, this time with all the positivity that you can muster.

If you find that remembering your affirmations is diffi-cult, pin them on your bathroom mirror so you can 'think' them as you clean your teeth. Write them on your shopping list or your diary. Each time you see them, say them to yourself two or three times – or as many times as you want.

Visualisations

Visualisations are the same as affirmations but instead of words you make mental pictures of the things you want. You need to create a clear picture of the object, person or situation exactly how you want it to be. Set this mental movie in the present, not the future; this way you will see things actually happening rather than waiting for them to happen. Include as many details as possible so that it is as real as it can be. As with affirmations, you should bring the picture to mind as often as you can and keep the thoughts that produce the picture positive and full of energy.

Visualisation should be a pleasant, uplifting process. The more you visualise your situation the more it will become part of your life.

Affirmations and visualisation are ways of thinking about your goals and achieving personal success. When you have been doing them for a while you will notice subtle changes in your attitude, as you begin to believe that anything is possible if you want it enough.

Both affirmations and visualisations are simple ways of turning your dreams to reality and giving substance to your innermost wishes. They enable you to confront dilemmas and fears; they reinforce the fact that you have been in a certain situation before and survived.

Day 27

CHANGE YOUR MOOD

Every day we are subjected to highs and lows of emotion. For no reason, you get up either in a good or bad mood – although by now you will be waking in a much better frame of mind than before! You are subjected to busy public transport; crammed supermarkets; late meetings; missed meetings; unhappy people; screaming children ... Each one of these stress factors will evoke an emotional response from you. Some of the responses will be positive: you realise you can learn from the incident, or you are able to turn it to your advantage. Realistically, though, some of the responses will be negative. You will be made to feel sad, or unhappy; or shocked; or melancholy; or distressed. None of these emotions can be positive or constructive and so you should find a way to change them as swiftly as possible.

Today is about finding out what can change your mood; what gives you an immediate lift from the negative to the positive.

- Deep breathing
- Loud music

- Quiet music

- Relaxation techniques

- Aromatherapy oils

- Bach flower remedies

- Friends

- Food

- Reading

- Exercise

- Walking

- Jogging

- Loud shouting

Any of these (or something else entirely) could be the trigger that can haul you back from the brink of a bad mood. You may already know that music is what you need to calm you down if someone has slammed the door in your face once too often. You may know that two drops of Bach flower rescue remedy and 10 deep breaths will wipe away the annoyances of the day. Many people find that a chunk of chocolate lifts the mood; or that half an hour in the sauna sweats out all the impurities and stresses of the day.

Try one or more of these 'calmers' each time something negative happens until you find the one that works best for you. Once you have found the correct technique, you should work out a way of having this 'cure' to hand at all times. A personal stereo in your briefcase or handbag with your favourite CD inside. Individually wrapped cubes of bitter chocolate so that you can have a small piece to lift your spirits without widening your waistline. A small joke book – the kind you get for Christmas and never know what to do with – tucked into your bag so that you can have a quick peep and a giggle. Four drops of Rescue Remedy on the tip of your tongue or dropped into a bottle of mineral water can serve as a calming tincture for moments of need. A quick walk around the block breathing deeply can be the required oasis of calm that stops any small niggle from becoming a big problem.

All these solutions are cheap or free of charge and can be used almost anywhere and any time. Simply knowing you have a solution to your mood swings 'on tap' may be enough to keep you calm and balanced; knowing that you are in control of the situation can stop you from having the change of mood in the first place. Try a few solutions and see which suits you best – then carry your 'calm kit' with you wherever you go.

Day 28

FLOATING DAY

Today is the last day to 'catch up' on anything you haven't had time to do yet and to reflect on all the things you have had time to do. Read your diary and remember the great things you have already achieved. Well done! Keep it up!

Day 29

YOUR PERSONAL MANTRA AND MEDITATION

Now that you have reached Day 29 you will be in a much more positive, detoxed frame of mind. Your thoughts are more focused, you are more open-minded and willing to share your ideas and inspirations.

Having a personal mantra or meditation is a bit like having a friend with you at all times. If things get too much to handle, or there is too much going on in your head, then saying your mantra or meditating can make life seem a lot less confusing and stressful.

Your mantras and meditations should be very personal, applicable to yourself, and your own needs. Your mantra should be easy to remember and short enough to repeat many times. It should be entirely positive, using only positive language. Just giving head-room to a negative thought or idea will give it credence.

If someone you know is going through a trauma then you can direct your mantra/meditation towards them by picturing them in your mind. If there is someone you dislike, direct your personal mantra towards them and your negative feelings will subside or will turn into positive ones – and make the person more bearable by giving you the strength to deal with them!

The language you use in your personal mantra/meditation should be accessible, simple to understand and unambiguous:

- May you be happy
  May you be healthy
  May you be safe
  May you dwell in peace

- I wish you health
  I wish you wealth
  I wish you success
  I wish you all the things you wish for yourself

- I am happy
  I am calm
  I am fulfilled
  And I am loved

- May you be calm
  May you be content
  May you relax
  May you be generous to others

Get the picture? Simple, short and easy to repeat.

Initially you should set a certain time in each day to say your mantra or to meditate; perhaps every morning upon waking, every lunchtime and then just before you go to sleep. As you become more used to saying your mantra you will find it easier to use whenever the occasion arises; for example you may talk to a friend on the telephone and, when the call is finished, replace the receiver and say the mantra a few times whilst the person is fresh in your mind. If you live away from your parents or loved ones, you can just direct your mantra at them, sending them your positive thoughts and feelings. If someone at work upsets you, just repeat your mantra for them – the positive thoughts will dispel the negativity of the specific situation. If you are about to go into an important meeting, picture yourself in the situation and repeat your mantra. This will calm you and put a positive image of how things will go into your mind. The picture will then become reality.

If you get to the end of the day and have not had an opportunity to say your mantra, you should find a quiet corner and say the mantra for yourself, to yourself, quietly. As you say it you should feel the vibrations of your words travel through your body like the ripples on a pond.

Mantras relax you. They help you to concentrate on the good things and eliminate the bad things.

I personally use a mantra to help me conquer my worst fear. I am terrified of flying. A few days before I am due to fly anywhere I start to take Bach Flower Remedies, which are very useful. But then an aromatherapist told me that, when I was actually on the plane, I should surround myself with calming white light and repeat my very own 'safety mantra'.

I start to repeat my mantra to myself both in the air and whenever I think about the flight:

I am happy
I am calm
I am safe and everything is fine

Originally I used to tell myself that 'I was safe and free from danger' – but a friend pointed out that 'danger' was a negative word and would only serve to put the concept of danger into my head! Since then I have used positive language only.

My mantra hasn't completely eradicated my fear, but it has made me much calmer. I am now much more able to settle into the flight – I don't feel compelled to sit watching the expressions on the stewardesses' faces, or listening for changes in the noise of the engine! Simply repeating my mantra can send me into a peaceful sleep; merely knowing that my mantra will work for me if I need it stops negative thoughts from taking control of the situation.

Day 30

A TIME FOR REFLECTION
Congratulations! Learning to congratulate yourself means
that you are acknowledging the effort you have put in and
the hard work you have done. No more worrying if you
are good enough – reaching the end of the programme is
proof that you are good enough!

You have now completed the *Detox Your Mind* programme.
Feel free to pat yourself on the back and banish all those
thoughts of doubt or questions of capability. Free your
mind to your success and indulge yourself in praise.

You have learned to look at yourself and love yourself.
You have found out about yourself and the world around
you. You are much more certain about what you want from
your life. You have made decisions about things that you
wish to happen and things that you don't wish to happen.
You have thought about where you want to go on a daily
basis and in the longer term. You have learnt to enjoy every
moment and not to wish away your days and weeks. You
have learnt to reject thoughts and ideas which aren't beneficial to you. You know how people see you and if you like
what they see and what to do about it if you want to change.
You have done this entirely on your own and you have
achieved in one month what most people don't even
approach in their whole lifetime. I think a feeling of self-
satisfaction is truly warranted!

Maintaining your clear head
You should consider maintaining your detoxed state of
mind. Carrying out tasks on a daily basis has been a strict

discipline for the last 30 days. Ideally you should continue to follow the programme, focusing from time to time on those challenges that bring your mind back into focus and back on line. This is easier to say than to do, I admit; you should look at ways in which you can continue the good work without following the programme each and every day. Perhaps you could carry out a task one day a week – or one day a fortnight.

What you will find is that your positive state of mind will remain with you until it is really put to the test! You will think you have cracked it – and then something will happen to shatter your positive outlook, and you will think you are back where you started. Don't worry – it isn't permanent. The problem is simply rectified. Just take a few deep breaths, and then think something positive or say something positive to change the situation and diffuse your tension.

Your diary has been very important during the programme but it is even more important afterwards as your support mechanism. Keep your diary close to hand; on your bedside table or in your bag. Each time you go to bed, have coffee or just have a free moment, turn to a page in your diary and remind yourself how you felt when you were detoxing your mind. Your diary will prompt you to recapture that feeling, to use a few of the tools that you learnt during the programme and put them into play at the next eventuality. If you start to feel as if your brain is filling up with 'clutter' or you are not getting the opportunity to be creative, flick through your diary and get back into your *Detox Your Mind* habits.

Even if you are managing to be positive and look after number one and you feel happy and contented, your experiences are still valuable. Your diary was your constant companion at a time in your life when you made tremendous personal changes – you should treasure it like a good friend. Like a friend, it will help you cope on the more 'difficult' days.

Maintaining creativity

Surprise yourself occasionally by asking yourself to 'draw' a person or scene that you know well – perhaps the same person or scene that you drew while you were completing the programme. Compare your efforts now with your previous drawing. Write a short poem about what is in your head – especially at times of high emotion. Draw how you are feeling. Do your creative efforts leave you feeling refreshed and energised, more in touch with your imagination and your feelings? Does your picture or poem tell you anything you didn't know about yourself? You will learn more about yourself every time you create something.

Take more risks

Go through your diary and remind yourself how you felt when you had completed your Perceived Risk task. Remember the exhilaration; the amazement; your determination to do something you feared. Remember how your mind and body helped you confront a situation you once thought impossible, Now you will be able to 'have a go' at anything, won't you? After all, you've done it once before ... You may wish to book another 'hair-raising' activity, just to keep your hand in.

Mental agility

Once a week or so you should recite the pieces of information you committed to memory: the PIN numbers, poem etc. If, by now, no effort is required to recall them you should find something new to learn to maintain that level of mental agility. Or why not take up quizzes – or cross-word puzzles? Fill in the crossword in your daily newspaper on the train into work each morning. Make sure you conquer new pieces of equipment and new technology as soon as you are faced with it. Keep your mind active; make sure it constantly assimilates new information. Reciting a list of new things that you have recently learned – or that you want to learn – every morning will wake up your brain and kick-start the day.

Forward planning

You should regularly revisit your 5-year plan to make sure that you are still on course. If something has been achieved, put a new goal in its place. Feel free to redraw your plan at any time if your circumstances change, but don't feel you have to present yourself with new goals just for the sake of it. Remember: a little movement every day towards your ultimate ambitions – no matter how small that movement may seem – will inevitably carry you in the direction of your big dream.

Planning for now

Remember to enjoy and fully experience everything that happens *now* – this moment. Now is the only thing that you can guarantee. Tomorrow is an unknown quantity – but you can rely on today. Get the most that you can from every moment of your life by opening yourself up to as many positive influences as possible.

Just think:

- If everyone you met was happy and confident

- If everyone was in a good mood

- If everyone had self-esteem

- If everyone had recently achieved a dream or achieved the impossible

- If everyone had put their problems into perspective

- If everyone went around smiling and laughing

- If everyone paid everyone else genuine compliments

- If everyone was aware of the needs of others

- If everyone cleared negative thoughts from their mind

- If everyone had just had a really good day ...

What an amazing place the world would be to live in!

Part 3

WAYS TO ENHANCE AND SUPPORT YOUR DETOX PROGRAMME

6

Brain Food

IT SHOULD COME as no surprise that the sorts of foods that are good for your brain, intelligence, memory, alertness and vitality are also good for you in lots of other ways!

Following a balanced diet will provide all the necessary nutrients to keep the mind alert and fit for the *Detox Your Mind* Programme. 'Balanced' is the key word here. Some foods we eat should be cut down, and some should be increased in order to fulfil all our nutritional requirements.

Fruit and vegetables and starchy carbohydrates should form about two thirds of our daily eating regime (one third fruit and vegetables and one third starchy carbohydrates). The remaining third should be made up of mainly meat/fish/protein with very small amounts of dairy and sugary/high-fat-content carbohydrates.

We should plan our mealtimes in order to be sure of having optimum energy levels when we most need them. Everyone has suffered the mid-afternoon-'snooze' syndrome when, after lunch, we are expected to carry on working when all we really want to do is curl up in a big comfortable chair and have a nap for half an hour. The importance of maintaining a continuous level of blood sugar is vital if we want to avoid any 'dips' of energy and brain function during the day.

The customary 3 meals a day may not be the best way to nourish our bodies and minds. Eating large breakfasts, lunches and evening meals will lead to a blood-sugar low before each of these meals as the body will have used all its energy. If stores become depleted directly before food is consumed, a blood-sugar high will occur directly after eating – which always results in another low an hour or so later, depending on the content of each meal (this explains the snooze syndrome!) If the carbohydrates consumed are carefully chosen, then the major peaks and troughs can be avoided.

During the *Detox Your Mind* programme you should ideally eat 5 or 6 smaller meals during the day in order to ensure the continuous levels of alertness required to fulfil your tasks. You should limit or ideally eliminate some foods from your diet during the programme as these are likely to inhibit correct absorption or release of some essential substances within your body. You don't want anything stopping you from getting the best out of all your hard work.

The best way to achieve optimum nutrition is to change your current eating regime to incorporate the required nutrients – simply taking supplements is a lazy way to change your diet.

'Everything in moderation' is a good piece of advice. If we binge one day and starve another we will suffer the consequences; if we drink very little fluid we feel dehydrated; if we drink too much alcohol one evening then we know the consequences the next morning.

There are some other rules that should be observed throughout the programme:

THE FOOD RULES

- Eat regular, small meals. Five or six small meals eaten regularly will keep you more mentally alert than two or three big meals.

- Eat breakfast. Low blood sugar in the morning adversely affects your memory and ability to concentrate. Breakfast will wake up your brain. If you try to work without first eating a small breakfast then your body is likely to ask for stimulants – short-term chemical solutions such as coffee, tea, sugar, chocolate etc. If you have breakfast then you will satisfy any needs and your mind can operate efficiently.

- Eat a mid-morning snack consisting of a slow-release carbohydrate. This will stave off any hunger pangs and keep energy at a constant level.

- Eat lunch as normal but make it light and refreshing – include lots of fresh, raw vegetables. If you do not like to combine carbohydrate and protein then you can still observe the combination rules; many recipes will naturally observe these requirements anyway.

- Eat a mid-afternoon snack to prevent the 'snooze' syndrome. Again, a healthy, slow-release energy food will make sure you don't create any problematic highs and lows.

- Supper in the evening should not necessarily be the largest meal of the day. Equal portions for breakfast, lunch and the evening meal will help keep your brain working efficiently.

A final snack before bed is fine, but make sure it doesn't contain anything that will prevent you from getting the best night's sleep possible. You will need every bit of energy to get you through the programme.

- Depending on your daily routine you should time your meals and snacks at equal intervals. If your day starts at 8.00 am then you should be thinking about taking your meals as follows:

8.30	Breakfast
11.00	Mid-morning snack
1.30	Lunch
3.00	Mid-afternoon snack
6.30	Supper
9.30	Light snack

  If you work somewhere that dictates your lunch hour etc, then obviously you will need to make the times more flexible. If your working day is much shorter or longer then the meals will be spread differently. But always try to make sure that the timings are split equally so that your body is not left without food for extensive periods of time.

- If you have ever suspected that you may be intolerant to foods such as wheat or dairy products then this is the ideal opportunity to exclude them from your diet.

- Try to keep your diet as natural as possible and try to cook the foods as little as possible. Vegetables should be raw, lightly stir-fried or quickly grilled to keep all the nutrients in them. Fruit is easy to eat raw and you should eat at least 5 pieces a day. Pasta, rice, bread and potatoes, grains, pulses etc should be cooked as directed but always cook so that you give your jaw a work-out – that means the goodness has not been completely boiled away. And you will get great muscle tone in your face from chewing!

Bad Nutrients

The following foodstuffs should be reduced or eliminated:

Caffeine You should limit your intake of any caffeine product to one drink per day – or cut them out altogether.

Alcohol You should limit your intake of any product containing alcohol to one unit per day – these units may not be 'rolled over'. One or no units per day is the maximum permitted.

Sugary products Cakes, biscuits, crisps, sweets, chocolate bars and all things 'naughty' should be eliminated or limited to one *small* slice/piece/packet/bar per day. These foods are high in calories and sugars and will give you a boost that will be swiftly followed by a drowsy 'low'.

Fats Products high in saturated fats should be avoided. Meat-fats and dairy-fats intake should be limited to polyun-saturates, oily fish, nuts and oils.

Smoking/Pollution Air-borne pollution and smoking – passive or active – should be avoided at all costs. If you smoke then give up now! And if you can avoid spending long periods of time in public areas that smokers use, or outside areas that have a heavy traffic or car use, then do. Smoking and pollution not only have the obvious side-effects of nicotine/passive smoking/addiction etc, but they also prevent complete absorption of vitamins and minerals from foods, they dull your taste buds, your skin tone and complexion will suffer and your general health will deteriorate.

Good Nutrients

Some foods are reputed to have a very positive, nourishing effect on our brains. I have listed these and then listed their natural food sources.* It is not advisable to take supplements to make up for deficiencies in your diet; it is much better to address your diet and make the necessary changes so that you incorporate those foods that were missing before and your body can assimilate them naturally. It is very easy to forget to buy various supplements and pills – but not very easy to forget to eat.

Choline	Aids memory	Vegetables, egg yolks
DMAE (dimethylaminoethanol)	Elevates mood, improves memory and increases intelligence	Fish, especially anchovies and sardines
Inositol	Nourishes brain cells	Grapefruit, cabbage
Niacin	Healthy nervous system and brain function	Liver, kidney, fish, eggs, poultry, avocado, peaches
Sulphur	Oxygen balance for brain function	Fish, eggs, cabbage
Zinc	Brain function and mental alertness	Wheatgerm, pumpkin seeds, eggs, ground mustard
Tryptophan	Essential amino acids for brain to produce serotonin	Milk, fish, turkey, bananas, dried dates, peanuts
Phenalalanine	Essential amino acid to improve memory and mental alertness	Protein-rich foods, soy products, almonds, pumpkins, sesame seeds
Carbohydrates	Glucose and blood sugar provide essential energy for our brain and central nervous system	Bread, pasta, pulses, rice, oats, potatoes, sweet potatoes
Iodine	Improves readiness and pace of brain	Kelp, onions, sea-food

* (Information taken from *The Vitamin Bible*, Earl Mindell (Arlington Books) and *The Optimum Nutrition Bible*, Patrick Holford (Piatkus Books).

Once again, I cannot impress upon you enough that a balanced diet will give you all these nutrients in the correct form. Taking supplements of any vitamins and minerals is not recommended unless you have first consulted a nutritionist or your GP. You may also wish to see a nutritionist if you are currently taking any prescribed drugs or the contraceptive pill; many medicines can prevent the body from absorbing essential nutrients or can deplete the body's natural stores.

BRAIN FOOD RECIPES

Having said that you should take all these supplements in their natural food forms, it is not always easy to find a way to include so many foodstuffs in your daily diet. Here are some recipes that will make sure that you get your fill of 'brain foods'. (Each recipe will serve one person – adjust quantities according to need.)

The recipes observe all the 'Food Rules'. They include as many raw vegetables as possible. The meals are portioned in small quantities in order to enable you to eat 5 or 6 meals rather than 3 larger meals. Many of the carbohydrates are slow-release ones so that you do not suffer from frequent highs and lows of blood sugar – helping you to maintain continuous levels of alertness and energy. No chemical stimulants have been used and, where possible, no preservatives or additives have been used. Some of the meals are also suitable as snacks. (Fruit is also very good for snacking on, but fresh is advised; often dried fruit contains very concentrated levels of sugar giving an unexpected blood-sugar surge.)

So: 'Bon Appetit!' to an enhanced memory, nourished brain cells, a healthy nervous system, mental alacrity and mental alertness!

BREAKFASTS
Fresh fruit salad with floral jus

Fruit salad has always been a good way to start the day. Early in the morning is the best time to eat fruit; it gets a clear run through the system without first fermenting on top of a meal. The floral *jus* adds a twist to the salad and can be added in any strength to suit your taste.

> Fresh fruit (try to choose bright, colourful fruit such as strawberries, oranges, apples, grapes)
> 1 tablespoon each of the following:
> Rose water;
> Orangeflower water;
> Elderflower cordial
> 1 teaspoon of honey

Chop the fruit into large chunks and place in a bowl. Make the *jus* by blending equal measures of the honey, rose and orangeflower water and elderflower cordial. A tablespoon of each is recommended the first time you make the blend but you can mix to taste thereafter. The honey and cordial provide the sweetness and the rose and orangeflower the 'floral' element.

If you want a really special breakfast to get you going, use sparkling elderflower 'champagne'. Add just before you serve and it will really enhance the flavours of the fruits.

Banana toast

This breakfast is brilliant to keep you going through the morning if you have a long meeting scheduled or it's your turn to look after the children.

2 slices of whole-wheat, granary or any unusual bread of your
   choice
1 ripe banana
Cinnamon to sprinkle

Lightly toast the slices of bread so that they are warm and a
pale golden brown. Peel the banana and squash the fruit
onto the toast. Sprinkle lightly with a little cinnamon (or
nutmeg) to taste. Toast again if you wish until the banana
has browned slightly.

Yogurt muesli crunch/Trail mix

The trail mix may be made up and stored in a container so
that you can use it for breakfast as a muesli. If you need an
energetic snack, a small handful of the mix will boost energy
until your next meal.

1 tablespoon each of the following: almonds; pumpkin seeds;
   sesame seeds; sunflower seeds; chopped dried dates;
   chopped dried apricots
1 small pot of low-fat yogurt

Mix the dry ingredients and store in an airtight container in
the fridge. When having the muesli for breakfast simply mix
the muesli with a small pot of low-fat yogurt – this crunchy
cereal will tone the jaw muscles as well! Carry a small bag of
the mix with you in your handbag or briefcase for extra
energy reserves.

Boiled egg and soldiers

Take a trip down Memory Lane and treat yourself to good old-fashioned egg and soldiers. Eggs are an excellent 'brain food' (but don't eat too many). Go to work on an egg!

1 egg
2 slices of brown bread

Boil the egg (3/4 minutes for a soft yolk; 6/8 minutes for hardboiled). Toast the bread and slice into thin strips – thin enough to dip into the egg if it is soft-boiled. Try not to add butter and salt; just taste the nourishment.

Banana fruit smoothie

Smoothies are usually a blend of fruit, fruit juice and milk or yogurt or ice cream. They can be as runny or thick as you wish. If you like to spoon your smoothie like a yogurt then use less fluid; if you like a really runny smoothie, add more juice or milk.

All the ingredients in a smoothie are to your own taste but ideally you should use 2 pieces of fruit to half a pint of milk or yogurt and 10mls of fruit juice.

Bananas
Peaches
Grapefruit
Fruit juices
Low-fat yogurt
Milk (if desired)

Blend the fruit together to make a creamy base. Add either fruit juice, yogurt or milk or a combination of these until you get the desired consistency. Add the fluid a bit at a time and mix thoroughly so that it looks appetising and not 'curdled'.

MEALS

All these dishes can be served as a main meal or a light snack. Just change the quantities to suit the occasion or appetite!

Jacket potato with roast onions and garlic peppers

Jacket potatoes are never the same when baked in a microwave but the speed element may be important. A good compromise is to cook them in the microwave until virtually ready and then put them in a very hot over for 20 minutes to crispen up – the best of both worlds.

- 1 large potato
- 1 white onion or 4 shallots
- 1 red onion
- 6 cloves of garlic

Bake the potatoes using your chosen method. Heat a baking tray in the oven with some sunflower or grapeseed oil in the base. Chop the onions into quarters – keeping the chunks really big means that there will be plenty of crunch left in the onions after cooking. Remove the baking tray and toss the onion chunks and the garlic cloves – unpeeled – into the oil. Place in the oven for about 15 to 20 minutes, until the onions have just started to caramelise and the garlic is soft but not burnt. Open the potato by scoring a cross in the top and squeezing it open; fluff up the flesh and then squeeze the contents of the garlic cloves into the potato. Mix together and then serve with the chunks of onion on a bed of fresh green salad – parsley will help your breath to stay fresh!

Salad Niçoise

Salad Niçoise is really popular and now we know why – it makes you brainy! This dish is so simple but looks as if you have spent days slaving over it – it's delicious too.

    1 fillet of fresh tuna or ½ 100g tin
    New potatoes, to suit appetite
    ½ red onion
    Anchovies, 3 or 4 to taste
    Green lettuce leaves (enough to cover plate)
    4 salad tomatoes or a handful of cherry tomatoes
    a handful of green beans
    Black olives to decorate
    Sunflower oil to drizzle
    Lime juice

This meal can be eaten hot or cold – the preparation is the same. If you are eating it hot, the timing needs to be observed quite closely.

Whilst the potatoes are boiling place the tuna steak under the grill. Grill the fish until golden but not dry and over-cooked – 5 minutes each side is suggested. Slice the onion into rings and shred the lettuce. Place the lettuce, onion rings, olives and cooked new potatoes, sliced in half, into a bowl and mix with sunflower oil and the juice of one lime.

Shake on to a plate and place the grilled (or tinned) tuna on top. Put the anchovies in strips over the salad mix.

Lemon Sardines on toast

This dish is very often served as a starter in restaurants but is equally as good as a main course if you use a couple more sardines.

    2 or 3 fresh sardines, washed and gutted
    1 lemon
    Sunflower oil to drizzle
    1 sliced tomato
    Freshly ground black pepper

Brush the sardines with sunflower oil. Place a few strips of lemon zest inside the fish and grill until cooked through. Slice the tomato and place on your plate; sprinkle with the pepper and place the fish on top. Squeeze with the lemon juice and serve with some chunky brown bread. (Try to avoid any butter as there is enough oil in the dish already.)

Avocado prawn salad

In fact, you can use any shellfish you wish.

    Ripe avocado with stone removed
    Fresh prawns/seafood/shellfish, peeled and shelled – cooked as
        per instructions or ready-prepared
    Lime juice
    Lemon Juice

Green salad
Rocket leaves

Peel and slice the avocado and mix in carefully with the seafood or prawns. Squeeze the lemon and lime juice over the salad immediately, to stop the avocado from turning brown. Serve the salad on a bed of fresh green salad leaves – rocket will add a slightly stronger flavour.

Garlic Sardines on toast

This meal is one step on from a snack, with all the flavours of a full-blown main meal.

3 or 4 fresh sardines, washed and gutted
2 slices of wholemeal bread
2 garlic cloves
1 tomato
Sunflower oil to drizzle

Take the sardines and grill until the skins are crispy and golden. Grill the toast lightly. Slice the garlic cloves in half and rub all over the toast slices. Slice the tomato and arrange over the toast. Place the sardines on top and drizzle a small amount of sunflower oil over the fish. Serve – and wait for your inspiration to come!

Lime & Ginger Fish

You can use any white fish for this dish as the colours and the flavour will make a unique combination of any choice. Monkfish is worth a try if you can get it fresh.

1 level tablespoon grated ginger
Lime juice and zest
1 fillet/steak of white fish
Watercress or spinach or a mix of green leaves

Take the fish, place in a bowl and grate the zest of the lime and sprinkle the ginger over the flesh. Leave for an hour in the fridge. Then grill the fish until just cooked through and slightly browned at the edges – this is likely to take 8–15 minutes depending on the thickness of the piece. Serve the fish on a bed of watercress and spinach leaves or a salad of your choice.

Bean and lentil salad

Mixed bean salads are very filling, have lots of flavour and will keep your energy levels high.

1 tablespoon of all or a selection of the following mixed beans
    and pulses cooked to their instructions: aduki; kidney; lima;
    pinto; green Puy lentils
1 red onion
4 peeled tomatoes
1 tablespoon sunflower oil
1 tablespoon balsamic vinegar
6 spring onions
Chives

Mix the cooked beans and pulses together and place in a bowl. Mix together a dressing of the sunflower oil, balsamic vinegar, chopped chives and sliced spring onions. Dice the red onion and tomatoes and add to the dressing. Mix together the beans and pulses and the dressing and serve with some hot new potatoes or a green salad.

Salmon with nut crust

The contrast of the succulent salmon with the crunchy fresh nut crust makes a nice change. You can use any fish you wish but oily fish is generally better as 'brain food' – salmon, tuna, mackerel.

1 fish steak/fillet
1 dessertspoon of each of the following chopped nuts:
    almonds; hazelnuts; cashews; brazils
Watercress
3 tomatoes

Grill the fish until just cooked – too much cooking will make the fish dry and lose all the flavour and texture. Crush the nut mixture in a pestle and mortar, or use a small bowl and the end of a rolling pin. The crush should be sufficient for the oil from the nuts to bind them together. When the fish is cooked place the nut mixture on the top of the fish and grill for a few moments until the nuts are beginning to brown. Serve immediately on a bed of sliced tomatoes with watercress, sprinkled with freshly-ground black pepper.

Hot lemon chicken/turkey with brown rice

A filling hot meal with can also be served as a cold salad if prepared in advance.

1 chicken or turkey breast
2 lemons
2 peeled garlic cloves
Grapeseed oil
Brown rice or wild rice
1 vegetable stock cube

Cut the chicken/turkey breast into strips and place in a bowl with the zest of 1 lemon, the crushed garlic cloves and a tablespoon of the grapeseed oil. Mix together and leave to marinate for at least 20 minutes.

Boil the rice for the required time, making sure that you remember to add the stock cube to the rice water to boost the flavour. Once the 20 minutes is completed, take the chicken/turkey and pan-fry or grill until lightly golden. While it is very important to make sure that poultry is cooked thoroughly, overcooking will result in dry, tough meat – watch it carefully! During the final grilling or frying moments, squeeze the remaining lemon juice over the meat. Serve on a bed of rice or, alternatively, toss the ingredients together and then make a light dressing of lemon juice and freshly chopped coriander to drizzle over your sumptuous salad.

Vegetable bread

This dish is a small savoury version of traditional bread-and-butter pudding: the method is the same, but the ingredients differ slightly.

1 small loaf of brown bread in thick slices – slice your own wedges rather than using sliced bread, which make the pudding soggy

1lb vegetables of your choice, finely chopped (broccoli,
    peppers, fennel, onions, etc)
2 eggs
¾ pint semi-skimmed milk
Black pepper
Grated cheese – mozzarella is beautifully stringy!

Chop your vegetables into fine slices, lightly fry until the
onions are translucent and the other vegetables slightly softened and put to one side. Chop your bread into thick slices.
Whisk the eggs and milk together and season.

Take an oven-proof baking dish. Layer the bread, cheese
and vegetables in that order until your baking dish is full
with a layer of bread and grated cheese on the top. Pour the
egg and milk mixture over the entire dish and then place in
the oven and bake for 30 minutes at 180°/350°/ gas mark 4.
This dish is filling served on its own, but you may wish to
prepare a tomato salad as a light accompaniment. Simply
slice some tomatoes, arrange on a plate, drizzle with olive oil
and season with black pepper and basil leaves.

Scottish fish soup

This dish is quite rich. It contains all the cooking fluids
with nothing thrown away, so all the nutrients and flavour
are retained.

½ pint semi-skimmed milk
2 potatoes
1 onion
1 fillet of fish (salmon, smoked haddock or mackerel)
1 knob of butter
Seasoning to taste

Put the fish in a shallow pan with the milk and poach until just cooked – for about 10 minutes. Drain the milk from the fish, but keep the milk! Remove all the bones and skin from the fish and break the flesh into medium chunks. Fry the onions in the butter and put to one side. Boil the potatoes in the milk from the fish and season. Once the potatoes are cooked you need to mash half of them into the milk mix to thicken the consistency – leave a few chunks of potato unmashed to make the soup more hearty. Add the fish and onions to the milk and potatoes and cook through until fully heated. Serve in large bowls. You can serve this dish with large bread croutons.

Seared liver with onion cabbage

If you like liver, then this dish is for you. The combination of all the dark, richly-coloured ingredients really concentrates the mind! The onion cabbage can be made in larger amounts, stored in the fridge and cooked to order; the amount below will make enough for several servings.

1/4 small red cabbage, finely sliced
1/4 small green cabbage, finely sliced
1 red onion
1 white onion
Portion of calves' liver

Shred the green and red cabbage. Lightly steam until just softened. Fry the white onions until golden brown around the edges. Grill the liver to your taste; some like it only just browned; but if you are like me it has to be really crispy and chewy. Mix the red and green cabbage and put on the plate, sprinkle with the cooked onions and place the strips of grilled liver on top. Decorate with the red onion chopped into rings. The dish is quite dry but can be made more moist if you fry the onions in oil and add this to the plate once they are cooked.

PUDDINGS

Peaches and roast almonds

As I said earlier, it is usually best to serve fruit for starters rather than as a dessert. However, there are times when you need to serve a pudding to round off a lovely meal, and these light dishes are just the job!

    2 peaches
    1 tablespoon of shredded almonds or crushed fresh almonds
    2 teaspoons of honey

Slice the peaches and arrange on a plate. Sprinkle with the almonds and then drizzle with the honey. Grill the plate (watching it continuously). The dish is ready when the peaches and nuts 'catch' around the edges. (NB: the honey mix will be hot, so don't burn your tongue.)

Roast bananas

This is even more simple than the peaches and roast almonds and looks and tastes just as good.

1 banana
Juice of 1 orange and 1 lemon
1 teaspoon of honey

Take the banana, place in the oven and roast on medium heat until the banana feels soft. The skin will blacken and should be removed before the skin actually splits. Boil the juice of the lemon and orange with the honey until they form a syrupy consistency. Take the bananas and split along one side, open the skin up and pour the citrus juice into the skin. Serve. You may want to indulge yourself and add *crème fraiche* or low-fat yogurt – or you can just have the fruity pudding naked!

7

Detox Therapies

ESSENTIAL OILS AND AROMATHERAPY

If you are going to take on the task of detoxing your mind then you should use all the available support and help you can get.

Aromatherapy and essential oils are one of the ways in which you can access this support at all times. The only evidence that you are using this form of therapy will be that you smell nice!

By looking at the origins of aromatherapy and the effects that essential oils can have, and how they are used, you will get some indication of how they can become an 'essential' part of your everyday life and, more specifically, an 'essential' part of your detox.

- The use of aromatherapy oils dates back to 3000BC. The Egyptians used oils for medical and cosmetic purposes as well as for embalming. The Greeks and Romans used them in medical practice. Mediaeval documents include many references to herbals and scented oils.

During the eighteenth and nineteenth centuries, substances such as morphine, caffeine and quinine obtained from plants were used medicinally. Even in the present day we still use plant extracts in common drugs.

Aromatherapy oils are not to be taken lightly. They can be dangerous if used incorrectly. They are not just fragrances, as some people believe; they are strong, effective drugs that can have both subtle and major effects on the body and mind. Use of oils should be treated with caution and should be under the instruction of a qualified aromatherapist or an approved instruction book or leaflet. Never choose an oil simply because it has a pleasant aroma; it may have side-effects or contraindications that can be harmful or dangerous. Make sure that it is the right oil for *you*.

The market has become much more aware of essential oils over the last few years and now many mass-produced products are available, making the use of essential oils much more safe and practical. Ready-made blends of essential oils; ready-made blends of bathing/massage oils; even ready-made *sprays* of essential oils to carry around with you and just spray as required. The element of doubt when using pure essential oils can be eliminated when using these blends, but you may wish to try using a small number of essential oils to create your own blends. But always follow the instructions.

There are many ways to use essential oils at home and you should try all of them over the 30-Day Programme, so that you can assess which is the most effective at speeding up the detox process and which best suits your lifestyle. After you have completed the programme you are likely to have 'found' some oils that you will keep with you always, to help you cope with any situation or give you an instant boost.

Aromatherapy/Essential oils and massage

When used at home without the instruction of a trained therapist, essential oils should never be applied directly to the skin without first being diluted. Essential oils are highly concentrated and can cause irritation or burning when applied undiluted or undispersed. (More than a ton of petals can be required to provide just 2mls of essential oil.)

Carrier oils or base oils can be used as a blend. Many of these are simply vegetable or seed oils that we use every day in our kitchens! This may seem a bit crude, but the oils are totally natural and therefore can be absorbed by the skin so they act as a moisturiser. Olive oil, sunflower oil, safflower oil, grapeseed oil, nut oils and sesame oil are all readily available oils that can be used in aromatherapy. Macadamia-nut oil, sweet almond oil, jojoba oil or avocado oil are slightly more exotic and can be found in natural health stores or some enlightened chemists. All carrier or base oils will effectively dilute the stronger, more potent essential oils which decreases the chance of skin irritation.

The ratio of any home-made blend of massage oils should be no more than 10 drops of essential oil to every 100mls of carrier or base oil. You should only blend sufficient oils for immediate use. Essential oils are a natural preservative, but if stored incorrectly the blend can become stale or rancid.

Find a plastic bottle or bowl and add the base oil. When you have chosen your desired essential oil, add it drop by drop to your base oil and stop when the blend has a sufficiently strong fragrance. Some oils are stronger than others and 2 or 3 drops will be sufficient. Always err on the side of caution. Use the blend as you would your normal massage oil.

Professional Massage
During an aromatherapy massage treatment the client is required to lie on a massage couch, either naked or in their

underwear and covered in towels or blankets for warmth. The practitioner will adopt a calm, relaxing approach. The treatment will usually last about an hour; you may feel drowsy after the session but a glass of cold water will soon remedy this.

When the massage is over, try to keep the oil on your skin for at least an hour as this will allow the essential oil to be fully absorbed. If you need to dress immediately after a massage then wipe any excess oil off before dressing, as it may colour or stain your clothing.

Aromatherapy/Essential oils and bathing

As with massage, essential oils should never be used for bathing without being first diluted in base or carrier oils. Alternatively, they can be dispersed in a dispersant. The two most readily available are milk or high-volume alcohol (vodka is best as it has no fragrance and no sugar residue). These products will break down the essential oil into much smaller droplets, which means the oil is more evenly spread in the water and is less likely to cause irritation to the skin.

Diluting your essential oil with a base or carrier oil will make your bath more oily. This is great if you can massage the residue of oil into your skin after the bath, but if you need to dress immediately after the bath then a dispersant is more practical. It will allow the oil to be immediately absorbed into the skin without leaving a greasy residue.

When bathing in essential oils you should not attempt to use soap, as this will destroy the effectiveness of the oil. Choose a time when you do not need to wash, ie just before bed or after you have already taken a quick shower. Run a bath that is hot enough to stay warm for 15/20 minutes but not too hot to be uncomfortable to sit in.

Choose either to dilute or disperse your essential oil. Whatever you choose – a dispersant or carrier oil – you need only fill a tablespoon with your chosen fluid. You should add no more than ten drops of essential oil to this.

When the bath is full, sprinkle the tablespoon of blended oil over the water. Close all windows so that none of the steam escapes; you might want to light some candles to create a really relaxing sensuous experience. Slowly get into the bath. Once submerged in the water, concentrate on breathing slowly and deeply, inhaling all the vapour of the oil. Allow your skin to soak and absorb the oils. You should be able to totally relax and unwind and to detox your mind!

Once you have finished the bath, get out slowly. If you have used a carrier oil, try to collect all the oil from the surface of the water on to your skin. Pat yourself dry, allowing as much of the oil as possible to stay on your flesh to act as a natural moisturiser. Any residual oil will continue to be absorbed.

Ideally you can now relax or go straight to bed!

Aromatherapy/Essential oils and inhalations

Using essential oils for inhalations is an excellent way to benefit from the oils without removing any clothing! By directly breathing in the vapour from the oils they will enter the olfactory system instantly, so attention should be paid to the amounts used. Boil some water and pour it into a large bowl. Add 2 or 3 drops of your chosen oil – no dispersants or carriers are required as the oil does not come into direct contact with the skin – and lower your head, covered with a towel or sheet, over the bowl. Inhale slowly through the nose and out through the mouth. You can lower your face closer to the water as you become used to the vapour. Inhaling is an excellent remedy for colds and coughs as the effects are immediate. Inhale for about 5 minutes, or until you have had enough, and then uncover your head and breathe the cool air.

You can also inhale essential oils by placing a few drops on an old handkerchief (the oils may stain) and holding the cloth near to the nose or mouth. Do not bring the cloth into contact with the skin as the oils may irritate.

Aromatherapy/Essential oils and compresses

There are some times when nothing more than a hot-water-bottle is required to relieve discomfort or pain or to simply give warmth and comfort. Using a compress is the aromatherapeutic answer to this.

Fill a large bowl with hand-hot water and add a couple of drops of your chosen essential oil to the water. Soak a large piece of cotton cloth for a couple of minutes. Then wring out the cloth and fold it into a compress large enough to cover the area of discomfort. Add 2 further drops of essential oil directly on to the compress (it will spread and dilute into the soaked cotton) and then hold the compress against the area of pain. You can use the compress until it cools down, then, if you wish you can repeat the process.

The compress is an ideal treatment for period pains, fever and headaches, though you can of course use it for any condition or any reason. A Lavender and Ylang Ylang compress (both oils for relaxation and rejuvenation) held against the forehead is a particularly soothing way to relax.

Aromatherapy/Essential oils and burners

Oil burners are an excellent way of dispersing essential oils into the atmosphere so that you can benefit from their therapeutic qualities whilst you go about your everyday business. (NB: oils should not be used when there are children under 5 in the room or house.)

The choice of burner is important; some look wonderful but are not very practical. You should choose one with a bowl that is big enough to contain 120mls of water. If the bowl holds much more than this it will take too long to heat; if the bowl is much smaller then it will burn dry before the candle has gone out. Fill the burner with water, light the candle below and then drop 4 or 5 drops of your chosen oil on to the surface of the water. It is actually difficult to use too much oil in a burner as the vapour is distributed throughout a large area, but if you start to develop a mild headache add more water or simply blow out the candle.

You could use dry burners: terracotta rings that fit round light bulbs, or electrically-heated porcelain plates. When a few drops of your chosen oil are placed on the heated surface, the heat causes them to evaporate, releasing the fragrance.

Aromatherapy/Essential oils and ready-made blends

Ready-made blends are the fast, commercial answer to using essential oils quickly, inexpensively and safely.

Colour

99% of essential oils are a clear light yellow colour. A few are darker – neroli and mandarin – and some, like lavender are very light, almost transparent. Very few are what we would call coloured and those oils are very uncommon. It is fair to say that most of the oils you come across for day-to-day use are light yellow. Carrier or base oils are the same; varying degrees of yellow to mid-brown. (Grapeseed is slightly greener and nut oils are very dark brown.)

If you examine the products available on the shelf you can use colour to help you decide how natural they are and how much essential oil they contain. If, for example, you want a relaxing blend for massage containing lavender and other relaxing oils, then the blend should be of neutral colouring, not bright blue or dark green. If you want a bath oil to invigorate, a bright pink or orange one is only likely to perk you up if you look at it not if you bathe in it! This is not to say that there is no place for these products. It is wonderful that people are being made more aware of the properties of aromatherapy oils and they make wonderful gifts. And if they encourage you to take a relaxing bath or have a massage then that can only be beneficial. However, if you wish to use essential oils for their specific, therapeutic qualities then you really should use the pure essential oil diluted in a pure carrier or base oil.

A to Z of essential oils/base oils for your 30-Day Detox

The following list is an A to Z of some readily available essential oils for you to use. I have also suggested how they might enhance your 30-Day Programme.

Almond Oil
Sweet Almond Oil is rich in protein and when used as a base or carrier oil can enrich your skin and combat dryness.

You may like to moisturise your skin each day during the 30 days with a small amount of sweet almond oil in place of your regular product; you should notice a difference using a natural oil within days.

Basil

Basil is one of my favourite oils. When I first went into business I used to burn this frequently in order to clarify my mind when making decisions. Basil is good for mental fatigue and can be a stimulant and tonic for your thought processes.

Clary Sage

Clary Sage can be used to aid muscle relaxation and relaxation from anxiety caused by mental stress.

Eucalyptus

Apart from all the bactericidal effects of eucalyptus, which are greatly beneficial at times of illness, this oil is greatly invigorating. It helps prevent mental fatigue so can be used as a burning essence to uplift and stimulate.

Frankincense

Frankincense is a very powerful oil; some people do not like the fragrance. However, it is very calming and can have a soothing effect on one's emotions. Particularly good for meditation.

Geranium

Geranium is a balancing oil. It is good for treating extremes of moods. Geranium acts as a hormonal balancer, so if you suffer from swings in moods due to hormones, it may help to smooth out those swings.

Hazelnut Oil

Hazelnut oil is packed with vitamins, minerals and proteins. It can be used alone or as a carrier or base oil with any of the essential oils listed in order to increase the benefits of your massage.

Jasmine

Jasmine is one of the most beautiful oils available to us and as you might expect – is incredibly expensive! However, you need only use a minuscule amount to receive the benefits and the fragrance is wonderful. On a therapeutic level, jasmine is a powerful anti-depressant and is often used when clients have developed self-loathing or self-doubt. Using jasmine will help you get in touch with your 'self'.

Lavender

Lavender deserves a whole book to itself! Here are just some of its properties concerned with mental stimulation or clarity: calming; soothing; balancing mood swings; reducing anxiety; increasing feelings of well-being; aiding sleep. Lavender is one of the most versatile and safest oils to use – if you only buy one essential oil then I would recommend lavender.

Mandarin

Mandarin, like many of the citrus oils, has an uplifting effect. Use it at times of self-hate, self-doubt and when you lack confidence.

Neroli

Neroli is used alongside rose and jasmine in cases of self-hate/worthlessness. Neroli can help with developing a positive state of mind and good self-esteem. It is expensive but, as with jasmine, the quantities required due to the strength of the oil are minimal.

Orange
Orange can be described as a 'poor man's' neroli. Positive self-image, state of mind and self-esteem are all qualities enhanced using orange essential oil.

Pine
Alongside basil, pine was the oil I used most at the start-up of our business. I had read somewhere that it 'enabled the user to throw off the burden of responsibility' – perhaps not the best state of mind for developing a new business, but it seemed to help at the time! Refreshing and stimulating it gives you a positive feeling – similar to the feeling of vitality you get after walking through a wood packed with tall pine trees.

Rose
Rose joins jasmine and neroli as the *crème de la crème* of essential oils: not just because its cost is high, but due to its wonderful qualities. It will certainly make you feel like a million dollars, which can be enough to change your state of mind to a more positive one. Rose is used in many eating disorders to encourage self-love and a feeling of worth. Rose will help you tackle anything the world can throw at you with a positive outlook.

Sandalwood
Uplifting, positive and a powerful aphrodisiac – what more do you need to conquer the world?

Vetiver
Vetiver is deeply relaxing and can be used if you are feeling stressed and anxious, or if you want a really good night's sleep.

Ylang Ylang
Calming, relaxing, anti-depressant and an aphrodisiac, ylang ylang has a wonderfully floral fragrance. If this is to your liking, then use sparingly; it can be extremely exotic.

The following emotional states can be heightened/induced by using these essential oils:

Self-**A**wareness	Neroli, Jasmine, Rose, Ylang Ylang, Geranium, Mandarin
Mentally **B**oosting	Basil, Eucalyptus
Cheerfulness	Rose, Basil, Pine, Ylang Ylang, Orange
Decision-making	Basil, Vetiver
Energising	Orange, Basil, Pine, Eucalyptus
Focus the mind	Basil, Ylang Ylang
Generosity of heart	Lavender, Rose, Geranium, Jasmine, Neroli
Happiness	All oils are good for happiness – the fact that you are using them will put you in a positive mood! Some particularly uplifting oils are: Rose, Orange, Jasmine, Geranium
Imagination	Free the mind with Orange and Jasmine.

Pine can be used to prevent you from rejecting the wilder ideas!

Joy	Neroli, Rose, Jasmine, Ylang Ylang
Knowing your mind	Basil
Self-**L**ove	See oils for Self-Awareness, Cheerfulness, Happiness and Joy
Motivation	Rose, Basil
Being **N**ice	See oils for Self-Awareness and Self-Love
Optimism/ being **P**ositive	Basil, Pine, Vetiver, Orange, Geranium, Frankincense
Calm and **Q**uiet	Lavender, Clary Sage, Mandarin, Neroli, Frankincense
Relaxing	Lavender, Jasmine, Rose
Stimulating	Basil, Pine, Orange and Eucalyptus
Thoughtful	Basil, Lavender, Rose, Frankincense, Vetiver, Ylang Ylang
Uplifting	Mandarin, Orange, Geranium, Rose, Neroli, Jasmine
Vitality	Basil, Pine
Wisdom	Rose
E**x**citement, **Y**outhfulness and **Z**est for life	Pine, Mandarin, Eucalyptus, Basil

My personal *Detox Your Mind* Essential Oil Survival Kit would contain the following oils. They should help you sail through everything you are likely to experience during the 30-Day Programme: Basil; Mandarin; Eucalyptus; Geranium; Lavender; Pine; Ylang Ylang.

RELAXATION EXERCISES

Relaxation is vital if you want to complete the tasks successfully and stay in a receptive, open frame of mind throughout the programme. The process may seem a little strange at first, but once you have carried out the exercises once or twice they will become quite natural. You can even make up your own personal relaxation sequence!

Lie in a comfortable position, with your back flat to the floor/bed/mat. If you have back problems, place a cushion under your thighs and knees to support your back. Place your arms loosely by your sides and let your legs flop open; make sure your shoulders are relaxed and your neck straight.

Start by scrunching every muscle in your body as tightly as possible, hold it for the count of four and then let everything relax into the floor. Check that you are breathing correctly to get the best out of the exercise (breathing technique coming soon!).

If you are using a relaxation tape then simply follow the instructions as they are spoken; if not, then something along the lines of the following sequence may be used. Read it through beforehand and then simply take your body and mind through the sequence in your own time. Don't worry if you can't 'learn' the sequence thoroughly. Just getting used to relaxing each part of your body and mind is what really matters.

Relaxation sequence

1. Close your eyes and start to breathe deeply in the manner described in the Breathing section of this book. After breathing correctly for a couple of minutes you should find that your breathing has slowed down considerably.

2. When you inhale, imagine that the air you are breathing in is warm and golden and is bathing your body in restful and positive light.

3. Now start to consider how your body is feeling. Start thinking about your feet and ankles. Are they tense? If so, relax them.

4. As you exhale, picture the air you breathe out as old, stagnant air, to be replaced by new, fresh air. Do this every time you breathe.

5. Think of your calves and knees. Picture the warm air moving around any tense muscles, bathing them in light.

6. Picture your knee joints and your thighs. Breathe deeply and relax.

7. Feel the air being breathed into the groin area, relaxing the tension and soothing the pelvis.

8. See the golden light swirling around your stomach and abdomen, cleansing and uplifting your centre of emotion and spirit.

9. Watch the light thread its way between each and every rib, filling the lungs and chest-cavity with warm, expanding air.

10. Watch each and every finger fill with golden light, spreading through your fingers and lower arms.

11. Breathe the energy into the shoulders and base of the neck. Feel the neck relax and melt into the floor.

12. Feel the light travelling into the root of every single hair follicle, making your scalp feel invigorated and tingling. Each time you exhale you are breathing out waste – each time you breathe in you are breathing in new life.

13. When you have renewed the life inside your body you should look to see where the source of your new breath and new light is coming from.

14. With your eyes still closed, look above you and see the beam of light shining down on your body. See it feeding into your abdomen. You are connected to this light. Breathe deeply and inhale all you need.

15. When you are ready, you can start to think about bringing your consciousness back into your own body.

16. Open your eyes slowly. If you are lying on the floor or bed, then roll over on to your side and wait a few moments before you sit up.

When you have become used to the above simple relaxation sequence you can progress to a more imaginative one. This sequence takes you to a place where you will find warmth, comfort and love. The same rules apply: get into a comfortable, supported position and commence breathing.

1. Close your eyes and imagine you are lying on the shoreline of a long golden beach. You are lying with your feet towards the water and your head relaxing on the fine, smooth sand.

2. As you are lying there, watch the golden sun beaming down on your body.

3. Look towards the light and see the shaft of sun connect between your centre and the centre of the ball of warmth and light.

4. Feel how the sun beats down and warms your every cell. Feel how your body drinks in the sunlight. The light is powerful and refreshing and it is flooding through your body.

5. Your breathing is deep and fulfilling. Now you begin to feel the water brush up and under your body as it lays on the sand.

6. The first little wave of water just touches your toes and the backs of your legs. As it returns to the sea it softens the sand below your body.

7. The next wave sends water under your body and up to your waist. Your body sinks into the sand as, once again, the water flows back into the sea – taking with it any tension and stress. Just feel it wash away.

8. The next wave comes up and under your shoulders and gently cools your neck. As it flows back towards the sea it takes all the tension away.

9. The next wave travels beneath your head. You feel your head sink into the sand and your hair moved and rinsed by the water.

10. Now you can focus on your whole body. You are cleansed and free of tension. The light is still focused on your centre and your body can take as much as it wishes. You can drink it until your body feels drenched in golden light – inside and out.

11. Now move your eyes to the sky and see the last drops of light drain into your body. The beam now leaves the sun and is absorbed into your body.

12. Start to move your hands and feet. Slowly move your limbs. Then roll over on to your side, rest for a moment and take some slow, deep breaths. Then open your eyes. Push yourself up into a sitting position and relax.

You are now full of light, energised, refreshed. Your body is nourished. You are ready for the day.

BREATHING

Breathing correctly will help you deal with every situation you will ever face. Deep breathing can calm and soothe; it can help you gather your thoughts; it can give you focus and concentration.

The following exercise will show you how deep breathing should feel:

1. Lie down and place your hands flat on your stomach with the tips of your fingers just touching.

2. To breathe correctly you simply need to relax your stomach muscles.

3. Inhale through your nose slowly for the count of four. Take in air until it feels like your stomach is full of air – this should make the tips of your fingers separate.

4. Pause for the count of four and then exhale through the mouth to the count of eight.

5. By feeling the air 'in your stomach' it shows that you have relaxed your diaphragm muscle which means your lungs have expanded and you have inhaled to full capacity. This will feel strange at first but it will soon become the 'normal' way to breathe.

If you feel yourself tensing up or getting nervous then taking ten deep breaths will get you back into a 'centered' position, ready to deal with the situation. You do not need to lie down to practice deep breathing, but the best way to learn the technique is to practise it lying down, with no restrictive clothing. Once you know how it feels to take in the full capacity of air you can breathe correctly all day long as you go about your everyday life.

MEDITATION

If you had to name the calmest people in the world, monks, Buddhists and yogis would be pretty high on the list; these people just glow with peace and calm. They seem unshakeable, unflustered, and this state seems almost impossible for we mere mortals to achieve.

As you detox your mind you are required to look inwards and try to achieve a small element of this peace and calm in your own mind. Meditation and yoga-style exercises will enhance this process. Moreover, they can be continued as part of your life long after you have finished detoxing and cleared your head.

The benefits of meditation are many. It aids deep and restful sleep; it keeps you calm and relaxed; it enables you to cope with difficult situations; makes you far more creative and inventive; it can increase your level of intelligence ...

Get your mat out! With benefits like that you would be silly not to give it at least a try.

Learning to meditate

Meditation releases tension, relaxes our systems and slows down the frantic brain activity which seems part of modern living. Meditation makes you focus fully on each and every moment. Everything that has gone before is irrelevant; everything that is about to happen is ignored. You stay *in* the moment, in a completely relaxed and unselfconscious state. Chilled out.

There are several types of meditation but the main two are Buddhist meditation and Transcendental meditation. Buddhist meditation is similar to positive thinking; it involves you thinking good thoughts and chanting mantras for the benefit of yourself and others. Transcendental meditation involves sitting in a single position and repeating a saying, phrase or even a sound until the whole body is at one, completely absorbed in the meditation process.

Whichever method you choose, meditation is perfect for the *Detox Your Mind* programme because it gives you a total sense of being yourself. You can focus on your own mind and body and concentrate on clearing your own thoughts until you are totally relaxed and at peace.

Learning to meditate takes a bit of effort. It is really hard to get into the habit of emptying your mind and looking inwards, even if it is only for 20 minutes a day. The best thing to do is to go to a class. These are often held at your local leisure centre or hall; alternatively you can call an association related to meditation and they will tell you where your nearest group meets. Joining a class is beneficial because it immediately puts you in touch with a group of like-minded people. And on a more serious note, attending a class will help you learn how to use the meditation properly to get in touch with your own thoughts. It may be that some fairly deep-seated troubles or worries are revealed when you meditate and having a trained teacher at hand can give the support that you need.

The discipline offered in a class will ensure that the techniques you use are fully understood. It won't be so easy to let your mind wander. A class will also help you discover the most appropriate position for you to meditate in. This is very important; you can hardly concentrate on your meditation if the whole time your legs are going to sleep, or your back is aching. The class will take you through the steps gradually until you feel happy to meditate on your own.

If you wish to try meditation at home on your own here are some important tips:

- Make sure your room is warm and quiet

- Choose a time when everyone is out and no one is due to call round

- Put the answerphone on or unplug the phone – if the call is important people will call back. Change your message to let people know you will be available in half an hour

- Practice a position that you can stay in comfortably for 20 minutes. You might lie on your back with your legs and lower back supported by a cushion. You may decide to sit cross-legged; this is sometimes helped by placing a cushion under your buttocks so that your pelvis is slightly tilted forwards and your back kept straight. You may sit upright with your feet placed sole to sole and your knees relaxed and resting on the floor. Your arms should remain by your sides with the palms facing upwards

- Decide on your mantra or chant. You may wish to devise your own mantra, or you could start by simply saying your own name, or humming the word OM

- Concentrate mainly on your mantra/chant and your breathing. Start by breathing deeply. Once you feel relaxed and comfortable and your breathing is slow, you should start to chant your 'sound' word slowly and softly until you feel its rhythm resonate through your body. Alternatively you can use the time to recite your mantra or affirmations. Consider each word as if it were a gift for yourself or a loved one

Your meditation should take only a short time each day. If you set out with the intention of meditating for an hour each day you will soon find other more pressing calls on your time. If, however, you choose to meditate for only 20 minutes, this will be much more practical to schedule. Everyone else can busy themselves having a cup of tea; or emptying the washing machine; or vacuuming the carpets; and after just 20 minutes you will emerge calm, relaxed, ready to take on the rest of the day. If at first your family doesn't appreciate you taking 20 minutes out, go ahead anyway! They will soon appreciate its beneficial effects upon you. Before you know it they will be booking you a full half an hour out each day, to make sure you get your meditation 'fix'!

YOGA

Yoga is the physical version of meditation. You use your body instead of simply your breathing to effect physical and mental change. Be warned: yoga is not a simple form of keep-fit exercise. Some of the advanced moves in yoga look as if they are completely beyond the bounds of human flexibility (they are quite possible if taught correctly, but you must build up to them). Attempting extreme yoga techniques without first learning the basics is like attempting long division before addition. Yoga is a discipline. It should be respected and practised regularly. Having a relaxed mind will help your body to 'work out' the moves; attempting them when stressed is likely to cause injury. You will find that after practising yoga for a while you will be able to find emotional, physical and mental calm very easily.

Yoga is physical and as such will tone your body but it will also tone your internal systems: respiratory, circulatory, lymph etc. It will also exercise your internal organs; some of the positions exert and release pressure on them and their surrounding areas. It will stretch your muscles, keep your joints supple and your spine healthy, supportive and strong.

Each yoga position has a special purpose and usually has a name. A yoga sequence or session will free all aspects of the body so that you achieve mental and physical clarity. Breathing into moves and holding them requires concentration and balance. There is nothing quick about yoga; getting your body into the positions safely and comfortably requires a process of gentle stretches, holding and concentration that means that you must focus 100% on what you are doing.

As with meditation, you should always start by having lessons with a qualified and experienced yoga teacher. The yoga class will consist of relaxation and warming-up exercises, followed by a series of positions that may take some time to achieve. These will be interspersed with further relaxation and balancing exercises. You are likely to need blankets, pillows and layers of clothes as the class moves through its various stages: still and meditative; physical work-out; tranquil and balancing. Always check what is required when you register with a class. And make sure the teacher knows your level; enrolling in an advanced class to begin with will prevent you from getting the best out of yoga.

Useful Addresses

The British School of Complementary Therapy offers a number of valuable courses and treatments:

Courses

Diplomas in Aromatherapy, Therapeutic Massage and Reflexology are available. Short courses in Indian Head Massage, First Aid and Beginners' Massage available and also workshops for Beginners' Aromatherapy and Stress Reduction and Management.

Courses are available for complete beginners through to professional practitioner level. All courses are fully accredited and externally examined. Successful students will be able to apply for insurance to practice and join all relevant professional bodies.

Most practitioner courses last from 9 months to a year and take place in the evenings and weekends. Daytime courses are also available.

The British School of Complementary Therapy also sells specially prepared aromatherapy blends ready for use – wonderful for helping with relaxation, mediation, cleansing and the whole *Detox Your Mind* programme.

Treatments

Aromatherapy, Massage, Acupuncture, Cranio Sacral Therapy, Shiatsu, Alexander Technique, Deep Tissue Sports Massage, Physiotherapy and Alexander Technique treatments are available.

For further information on treatments, courses and oils, please call 0171 224 2394. We will be pleased to send an information pack at your request.

Jane Scrivner can be booked directly for Massage treatments and LaStone Therapy treatments at her clinic in Stratford Upon Avon on 01789 264141 or alternatively can be contacted on 07171 224 2394 for occassional London treatments.

The organisations below will help you find a qualified practitioner practising that particular therapy in your area:

British Complementary Medicine Association
9 Soar Lane
Leicester
LE3 5DE
0116 242 5406

Institute for Complementary Medicine
PO Box 194
London
SE16 1QZ
0171 237 5165

Aromatherapy Organisations Council
3 Latymer Close
Braybrooke
Market Harborough
LE16 8LN

British Acupuncture Council
Park House
206–208 Latimer Road
London
W10 6RE
0181 964 0222

The Edward Bach Centre (Bach Flower Remedies)
Mount Vernon
Bakers Lane
Sotwell
Wallingford
OX10 0PZ
01491 834678

Colonic International Association
16 Englands Lane
London
NW3 4TG
0171 483 1595

Association of Reflexologists
27 Old Gloucester Street
London
WC1 3XX
0990 673320

Transcendental Meditation
Freepost
London
SW1P 4YY
0990 143733

Yoga for Health Foundation
Ickwell Bury
Ickwell Green
Biggleswade
SG18 9EF

The Research Council for Complementary Medicine
60 Great Ormond Street
London
WC1N 3JF
0171 833 8897

Aromatherapy Trade Council
PO Box 52
Market Harborough
Leicester
LE16 8ZX
(Send SAE for Information)

School of Meditation
158 Holland Park Avenue
London
W11 4UH
0171 603 6116

The Shiatsu Society
31 Pullman Lane
Godalming
GU7 1XY
01483 860771

Iyengar Yoga Institute
223a Randolph Avenue
London
W9 1NL
0171 624 3080

Metamorphic Association
67 Ritherdon Road
London
SW17 8QE
0181 672 5951

T'ai Chi Union for Great Britain
23 Oakwood Avenue
Mitcham
CR4 3DQ

Index

THE BRITISH SCHOOL OF COMPLEMENTARY THERAPY.

140 Harley Street, London W1N 1AH 0171 224 2394

On production of this coupon you are entitled to 20% off any course or treatment you book in either London or Stratford Upon Avon. Massage, Aromatherapy and Reflexology treatments are available to combine with your detox programme.

Brochures of treatments, courses and dates are available on request in writing to The BSCT, 140 Harley Street, London, W1N 1AH.

NB; keep this coupon until any payment is required and reduction will be made at time of purchase. Do not send with brochure request.

Please send a copy of your brochure to:

Name ....

....

Address ....

....

....

....

Telephone No. (H)...........................(W)...........................

Send to: The BSCT 140 Harley Street, London, W1N 1AH

Also by Jane Scrivner

DETOX Yourself

FEEL THE BENEFITS AFTER ONLY 7 DAYS

✓ Banish cellulite
✓ Increase your energy levels
✓ Boost your immune system
✓ Lose weight
✓ Improve your complexion

JANE SCRIVNER
British School of Complementary Therapy

0 7499 1766 0   £6.99

Detox Yourself is an easy-to-follow,
highly effective spring-cleaning
programme for the whole body.
Follow her simple advice and in
only seven days you'll really
notice the difference!